FINDING GOD
in the *face* OF
EVIL

FINDING GOD
in the *face* OF
EVIL

ED DOBSON

kregel
PUBLICATIONS

Grand Rapids, MI 49501

Finding God in the Face of Evil

© 2002 by Ed Dobson

Published by Kregel Publications, a division of Kregel, Inc., P.O. Box 2607, Grand Rapids, MI 49501. For more information about Kregel Publications, visit our Web site: www.kregel.com.

Cover photo: Graham Morrison/AP/WWP
Cover design: John M. Lucas

ISBN 0-8254-2458-5

Printed in the United States of America

1 2 3 / 06 05 04 03 02

The LORD reigns forever;
    he has established his throne for judgment.
He will judge the world in righteousness;
    he will govern the peoples with justice.

The LORD is a refuge for the oppressed,
    a stronghold in times of trouble.
Those who know your name will trust in you,
    for you, LORD, have never forsaken those
        who seek you.

Sing praises to the LORD, enthroned in Zion;
proclaim among the nations what he has done.
                —Psalm 9:7–11

CONTENTS

INTRODUCTION

TWO WEEKS TO THE DAY after September 11, 2001, when the World Trade Center Towers fell, I met with a group of evangelical pastors in New York City. We all struggled to find a response to the crisis. Our struggle was that shared by New Yorkers, people in Washington, D.C., and millions more around the United States. The murderous attacks had stirred spiritual and emotional suffering of such magnitude that only God could get his arms around it.

As the morning passed and the discussion intensified, one of the pastors, Michael Faulkner of Central Baptist Church, spoke. "Brothers," he began, "everything has changed. The whole paradigm of ministry has shifted. What we did before 9-11 is no longer relevant. Everything is new!"

His words proved to be prophetic, for some weeks after September 11, people were more willing than they had been for decades to look to the church for answers to ultimate questions in their lives. On the Sunday after the Towers fell, church services across North America were packed. In my own church's sanctuary, people crowded the aisles and even sat on the steps to the platform. A serious mood hung over the congregation— people had come to hear from God. Their minds were scorched with images of destruction and filled with a multitude of conflicting thoughts.

Over the months that followed, the crowds diminished but the seriousness of the questions raised didn't go away. Often in a crisis people are concerned for a few weeks, then everything returns to normal. But this time a different quality of thought lingered. As the rescue workers continued to sift through the rubble, an entire generation seemed to be carting off some of the junk that lay in crumbled ruins in their minds and hearts. People were trying to make sense of what happened. I've never in my entire ministry seen people so open to spiritual matters, never seen such a hunger to understand the Bible, to understand where God was on September 11, and to understand where he is today.

Churches across the country spent weeks dealing with the aftermath of this crisis. We dealt with it through the rest of the year. I continued to remember those words of Michael Faulkner: "Everything has changed. The whole paradigm of ministry has shifted." But how precisely has the change affected us in ways that count? As I struggled through those thoughts, a series of sermons emerged, and those sermons eventually grew into this volume. The chapters ask the questions that I was asked over and over. It is not the intent of this book to give exhaustive theological discussions in response to each question. Rather, it seems that now is the time for basic and practical perspectives that are drawn consciously from God's Word.

So, although this book doesn't take us to a vantage point from which we can see all of the final confrontation between God and evil, it will show the basic geography of the field of conflict.

chapter one

What Stares Back When We Look Disaster in the Face?

He who dwells in the shelter of the Most High
    will rest in the shadow of the Almighty.
I will say of the Lord, "He is my refuge and
    my fortress,
        my God, in whom I trust."

Surely he will save you from the fowler's snare
    and from the deadly pestilence.
He will cover you with his feathers,
    and under his wings you will find refuge;
        his faithfulness will be your shield and rampart.
You will not fear the terror of night,
    nor the arrow that flies by day,
nor the pestilence that stalks in the darkness,
    nor the plague that destroys at midday.
                        —Psalm 91:1–6

WHERE WERE YOU on September 11?

I pulled into the car dealership for an oil change. I had no more than found a place to park when a friend who works there ran out to meet me: "Come into the waiting room," he said. "Look at the TV!"

About a dozen people were huddled grimly around the set, and I got there just in time to see the second plane slam into the second of the two World Trade Towers buildings.

The reporters didn't know many more facts than did those on our side of the television screen, but already they voiced vague suspicions about the possibility of terrorism. The people in the waiting room were speechless as they watched replay after replay of the planes smashing into the Towers. I remained glued to the television until my car was ready. When I got into the car I immediately switched on the radio, only to hear that yet a third plane had crashed, this time into the Pentagon. There were reports that a fourth plane was off course and headed in the general direction of Washington, D.C.

How could any of us focus on work responsibilities in the midst of the breaking developments? I tried, but I kept going back to the television to learn more. It was hard to keep up. The President of the United States and the leaders of Congress had been transported to a secure location; the White House had been evacuated.

It was a day of chaos unlike any other in American

history. The very speed with which information was collected and disseminated made this man-made disaster somewhat different in its personal toll than that faced on December 7, 1941, the occasion that begged comparison.

Our church leaders decided to call an evening prayer meeting. Information about the event spread by word of mouth, and more than a thousand people came to pray that night. Astounded, we planned further prayer opportunities through the rest of that week. Each day's attendance was in the hundreds. Those who prayed continually expressed the shared thought that we were experiencing at that moment one of the defining moments of our lives. Only after the passage of a few more months have events begun to clarify our perspectives as to just how life-changing September 11 was. Social historians will be looking closely for years to give a fuller report on what this one morning did to our patterns of thinking.

Even now, a few months after the World Trade Center was erased from New York City's skyline, I cringe when I see pictures of Manhattan Island. New York has for years been my favorite city in the whole world. I still see the city through an immigrant's eyes as the gateway to a new and wondrous land. It was in 1964 that my family left our homeland of Ireland and made the crossing to a new life in the United States. We crossed the Atlantic Ocean on the Queen Elizabeth and sailed into New York Harbor on a crisp morning in September.

What an adventure for a child was mine as I stood on the deck of the oceanliner in the early morning darkness with my sister and parents. I had never conceived of anything so massive as the New York City skyline. That city would continue to shape my life and ministry.

My first thoughts that God was calling me to a life of serving him in pastoral ministry came during high school. I was part of a Bible study in Harlem with converted gang members. Not many years later, I learned to preach on the streets of New York City. Tom Mahairas and I spent a good part of one summer learning by doing evangelism in that tough environment. While he preached, I handed out literature. Then I would pass the tracts to him and open my Bible as we reversed tasks. We'd stay on the streets until three or four in the morning.

Yes, I love New York as only one can who has felt its embrace. Many years later, parts of my heart crumbled as I watched the Trade Towers fall. It seemed like a very bad dream.

Evil up close and personal

During the week that followed the disasters, a great many of us Americans became almost addicted to TV newscasts, living from sound bite to breaking special report. I'd try to move on to other things and turn off the radio and television. Not long afterward, I would wander back to the remote control, checking to see if there were any new developments. How many times could you watch replays of a plane slamming into the side of a skyscraper and buildings collapsing, knowing that men and women were in the midst of the steel and concrete? I grew sick of watching the horrific images over and over. No, I would not again stare at the screen and watch those awful fatal seconds. But there it replayed again, and my eyes had remained fastened on the deceptively graceful descent of 110 floors into ruin. I couldn't turn away. I felt as if I was standing on the street of my own hometown of Grand Rapids, Michigan, watching history unfold before my eyes. It was as if my heart lay buried under hundreds of tons of rubble.

My street-preaching friend Tom Mahairas still ministers in New York City as president of the urban ministry supporting CitiVision, alongside Mike Faulkner, pastor of Central Baptist Church. One week after September 11, it was time to visit them and make a convalescent call upon my former and dearly beloved city. Our Grand Rapids congregation wanted to be involved in doing something, but how could we best help? Carlos Hidalgo, the chairman of our church board, accompanied me as we went to learn more. Like me,

Carlos is a New Yorkophile who worked for many years with a major advertising agency in the city.

We arrived on Sunday afternoon, and Tom met us at the airport. LaGuardia crawled with security. After a supper in Greenwich Village, we drove into Manhattan, parked, and walked toward Ground Zero. Again, security was incredibly tight. Every block someone in uniform stopped us, demanding to see picture IDs. We walked down the middle of thoroughfares that had been the private speedrome of cabbies only days before. Now streets were eerily empty, except for dust and debris.

As we approached Ground Zero, my emotions were overwhelmed at the sheer magnitude of devastation. Smoke rose from a ten-story-high jumble of debris. It was midnight, but the glare of work lights flooded the area, turning night into day. Hundreds of rescue workers picked through the smoldering gray. Truck after truck was loaded with twisted steel and concrete to be hauled away. It was New York City, and we were surrounded by people. Yet an unearthly silence enveloped the scene—no one talked. All that could be heard was the drone of heavy equipment. I tried to take it all in, but my mind couldn't come to terms with the enormity of the reality that this burial ground for thousands had been the proud hub of world banking and commerce.

Some time later, several police officers walked by. A pastor accompanying us asked the officers if they'd like to pray. One does not, as a matter of protocol, ask on-duty New York police officers to pray. Here the response was warm and immediate. Yes, they immediately responded, they would like to pray. We gathered in a circle, then opened ranks for two more who were walking by in their gas masks. Our arms were linked around one another. Someone asked me to pray.

Long moments of silence passed. I could not get a word out. The preacher who stands to pray before many hundreds each Sunday, who is never at a loss for words, stood with arms around police officers in what looked like the midst of Armageddon. What does one say before the throne of God at such a moment? I simply didn't know.

I prayed. I said something—what it was I have no idea. I learned that in such a moment, embarrassed silence before the sovereign Ruler of all things may be the only proper response.

Struggling for meaning

The next day we again made our way to the site. Mike Faulkner had arranged passes, a scarce commodity, because security was tightening even more around Ground Zero. To obtain our permits, two police officers escorted us to the National Guard center established near the site. Guards stopped us as we walked in, asking us to present photo IDs. Even the armed police officers in uniform had to produce photo IDs in addition to their badges.

After receiving the official badges, we headed to the site. The National Guard manned all the checkpoints, and at every block, someone in uniform stopped us and we had to show our badges and photo IDs. I was beginning to see that life had changed in America. Having grown up in Northern Ireland, I understood tight security and was accustomed to seeing heavily armed soldiers on the streets. But I had never seen such a military presence on the streets in America.

My feelings at seeing the site in daylight were no different than they had been the night before—I was overwhelmed. Even the rescue workers, who put in long shifts day after day, could not become hardened to the setting. We passed a rescue team trudging back to the support area to take a break. Their faces wore blank expressions. I could only imagine what they had seen. Although rescuers still hoped that people would be found alive, those hopes were fading. And that diminishing hope showed on the faces of those brave men and women who methodically worked through the wreckage.

We circled the site of about twenty-three acres, noting not only the immediate devastation but also the heavy damage to surrounding buildings. We passed a restaurant where the windows had been blown out. Inside, plates and glasses still decorated the tables as if the next party of customers would be seated momentarily. On a wall, a painted sign read, "You never know what is around the next corner." Just beyond the sign was the future that we had not expected to face around the next corner—Ground Zero.

Tears filled my eyes as I reached the temporary memorial to the fire fighters. They came again as I looked over the pictures of the missing, and read notes of encouragement from children that had been posted there.

As I absorbed it all, everything else in my life seemed to shrink in size—the problems of pastoral ministry, my own personal disasters. In the face of such immensity, our individual momentous experiences take on a far different meaning. It dawned on me that over several hours I had seen hundreds of people at work, but not one of them was smiling. There was nothing to smile about.

Back home in Grand Rapids, it is no easier to express what I saw on those twenty-three acres of Manhattan real estate or to explain its significance. To this day, as I try to describe it, the words simply do not come out quite right. Even attempting to put this sort of event into words seems inappropriate. I have seen the result of history's single most enormous act of terrorism. I have stood on consecrated ground—the unmarked graves of thousands who suddenly and irrevocably were pulled from their daily routines into the presence of God—and I will never be the same.

Since my visit to Ground Zero, I've preached about the tragedy and struggled through God's answers to the questions—questions from others as well as questions that I have been asking.

Personal towers also fall

In God's timing, I had begun to face some of the questions before September 11, 2001. My trip to New York came after a year in which my personal life had been rocked by disaster. America changed on September 11, and the day my life changed also fell on a beautiful day in autumn. The sun and clear blue sky beckoned me to play nine holes of golf, but instead I sat in the consulting room of a neurologist, waiting for the results of my examination.

As I waited, I anticipated hearing that something was seriously wrong inside my body. For several years, I'd noticed a weakness in my right hand, especially when twisting the lids off of jars. I'd lost some strength in other muscles as well. Well, I certainly wasn't getting any younger. These things happen. Then I noticed that I was feeling more and more sudden twitches in muscles all over my body. My wife, Lorna, continually encouraged me to see a doctor. I ignored the symptoms and her advice until one day when I was writing my sermon notes. Suddenly my hand would not cooperate with my brain. It was as if the hand was half a step behind what it was being told to do. That was a frightening moment, so the next Sunday I stopped a neurologist friend after the service and confided what had happened.

"You'd better come see me," he said, "like tomorrow!"

After my wait, the doctor came in and sat behind his desk. "There's something wrong," he began, choosing his words carefully. "I suspect motor neuron disease."

He hurried on to qualify what he had just said. "There's a continuum of motor neuron disease. On the one end, there are benign fasciculations—those muscle twitches you've been experiencing. Everyone has them but some have more than others do. What you have may be benign, in which case you just have to learn to live with it. At the other end of the continuum is ALS, or Lou Gehrig's disease."

When I heard ALS, my heart sank. I knew about amyotrophic lateral sclerosis. I'd visited every month with a young man in our church, who had died after fighting ALS for seven long years. I had also visited a man who had lived for about a year after his diagnosis.

The doctor let what he had said sink in, then he continued. "I'll arrange for some tests at the University of Michigan neuromuscular clinic in Ann Arbor."

As I left the neurologist's office I knew that my world had changed forever. I was hoping for the best—the benign muscle twitches that would be no more than a nuisance—but I dreaded the worst. The month that passed before my clinic appointment was an emotional roller coaster. I spent hours on the Internet, researching ALS. Sometimes I was sure I didn't have the disease. Sometimes I was sure that I did. As I continued with my pastoral work, preaching and visiting, I carried an unshared burden of fear.

At the clinic, the first part of my appointment consisted of a full physical examination. The doctor tested the strength in all my muscle groups. When he got to my right hand, I knew something was wrong when he asked me to resist as he pushed down on my fingers. I tried, but to no avail. I couldn't resist his pressure as I could with my left hand. For the first time, I knew with some certainty that something was seriously wrong.

They sent me for blood tests and a test in which a needle is poked into the muscles, while sophisticated instruments record what happens. The results of this rather unpleasant procedure show whether there is neuron damage. The test confirmed that there was neuron damage in my right hand and arm. There also were fasciculations, twitches, in all of the other muscles tested.

Further tests ruled out various diseases that mimic motor neuron disease. If those tests came back negative, then it was likely that I had ALS. I had learned that I had the basic symptoms of ALS—muscle atrophy, neuron damage, fasciculations, brisk reflexes. But the actual damage was confined to the right arm. Unless it spread I didn't meet all the criteria for a confirmed diagnosis. The only way to know for certain whether one has ALS is to observe the progress of the disease over time. I was to return in three months for further testing.

This was disheartening news. I was hoping to at least get to the bottom line immediately, and had held out continuing hope for a favorable diagnosis. Now I'd have to wait another three months to have *any* kind of diagnosis.

Three months later I went back, and the tests showed little progression.

"We still think it is ALS," I was told, "but you need to come back in nine months."

Nine months later I was back for my third set of tests. They again showed little progression by the disease.

"You have all the signs and symptoms of limb onset ALS," the doctors told me. "We want to see you in another six months."

And so the journey goes.

It is part of pastoral ministry to help many people through their personal disasters. I know what to say, know the promises of Scripture, know about prayer.

What I didn't know until the moment of the diagnosis was the immense chasm between knowing about disaster and actually going through disaster. The difference is like descending from daylight into darkness.

Today in Israel a first-century tomb can be visited in Bethany. It is alleged to be the tomb of Lazarus. A small door opens at street level. Visitors go down a spiral stone staircase to an underground cell. After crawling under a boulder, visitors arrive at a burial cave, complete with shelves on which the bodies were placed. The tomb is dark, cold, damp, and claustrophobic— far from the warmth of the sun.

Learning that I had a terminal and irreversible disease felt like that tomb. I'd left the warmth of day and slowly descended into a cold and lonely place, isolated, in darkness, confined to a prison, far from the sun, far from the Son. No prayers would make this diagnosis and its implications go away. No Scripture verses came to mind that could lift me from the crypt. There was only the challenge of getting through the next day. Some days were better than others, but every day was a struggle.

I am now much farther down the road, and the warmth has returned. Most of the time I'm out of the tomb, but I still face challenges. And after September 11, I see even more clearly that disasters come in a variety of forms. But whether they come in falling towers or fatal illness, we all have the same questions and issues. We all cry out for comfort:

> Be not far from me, O God; come quickly, O my God, to help me. . . . But as for me, I will always have hope. . . . Do not forsake me, O God, till I declare your power to the next generation, your

might to all who are to come. . . . Though you have made me see troubles, many and bitter, you will restore my life again; from the depths of the earth you will again bring me up.

—Psalm 71:12–20

The Bible doesn't give all the answers, of course. But it does give us a framework for coping with struggles for the next mile, even when the living is forever altered.

chapter two

WHERE IS GOD WHEN DISASTER STRIKES?

I heard and my heart pounded,
    my lips quivered at the sound;
decay crept into my bones,
    and my legs trembled.

Yet I will wait patiently for the day of calamity
    to come on the nation invading us
[or "for the nation to arise who will invade us"].

Though the fig tree does not bud
    and there are no grapes on the vines,
though the olive crop fails
    and the fields produce no food,
though there are no sheep in the pen
    and no cattle in the stalls,
yet I will rejoice in the LORD,
    I will be joyful in God my Savior.

> The Sovereign LORD is my strength;
>   he makes my feet like the feet of a deer,
>   he enables me to go on the heights.
> —Habakkuk 3:16–19

ANY TIME THAT WE find ourselves standing in the middle of a disaster, the initial shock is followed by questions. When the terrorists attacked America on September 11, 2001, I wondered what to say about the crisis the next Sunday. Dan Kregel, the pastor of student ministries, surveyed some of the high school students to find out what questions they would like answered concerning the attack. He spoke to about seventy students, and some of their questions inspired portions of this book. Their questions included these:

- If I join the armed services, is it wrong to go and fight?
- What are we going to do to get justice?
- Are we supposed to love the terrorists?
- Why did God let this happen?
- How could some people hate us so much?
- Why is the United States so vulnerable?

Two questions in particular came up again and again. Nearly one-third of the total questions concerned the last days: "Is this a sign of the end of the world?" The next most frequently asked question was about God:

"Where was God in all of this?" This last question is one that comes to mind whenever we face disaster: "Where is God?"

Disaster and God

Two major themes in the Bible deal with the issue of disaster and God. First, Scripture tells us that God is in control.

> He is the image of the invisible God, the first-born over all creation. For by him all things were created: things in heaven and on earth, visible and invisible, whether thrones or powers or rulers or authorities; all things were created by him and for him. He is before all things, and in him all things hold together.
>
> —Colossians 1:15–17

The text says he holds all things together—not just a few things, not just the good things, not just some things. God holds the entire universe together, being involved in the affairs of history and the disasters that happen to us all. God is never caught off guard by disaster, no matter how suddenly it occurs or how large and terrible its consequences. He never calls a cabinet meeting to discuss how he will respond to tragedy, nor does he sit in heaven, pondering what he will do next.

Our knowledge that God is in control, however, raises a number of questions: Is God, then, responsible for evil? Is God directly involved in all tragedies and disasters?

These are valid questions, and they will be addressed in the next chapter.

Evil and free will

The second major theme in the Bible, relating particularly to disaster of the man-made variety, is that humans have free will. As humans, we are agents who are allowed to make moral choices. Consider the first humans, Adam and Eve:

> The LORD God took the man and put him in the Garden of Eden to work it and take care of it. And the LORD God commanded the man, "You are free to eat from any tree in the garden; but you must not eat from the tree of the knowledge of good and evil, for when you eat of it you will surely die."
>
> —Genesis 2:15–17

The key word in this passage is *free*. Humans were created with free will. God could have created preprogrammed automatons who would respond to his commands, but he chose to create us with the potential for doing either good or evil. On September 11, the terrorists who hijacked the planes chose to do evil; the fire fighters and police officers who rushed into the buildings while others rushed out chose to do good and to display extreme self-sacrificing courage. The passengers in that fourth airliner, who tried to wrest control of the plane from the hijackers and thwart the terrorist plan, made a brave choice to fight. They chose death in the act of doing good as they forced the terrorists to crash the plane in Pennsylvania where it would do no harm to others.

In the aftermath of the September 11 disasters, people from all over New York City, Washington, D.C., and Pennsylvania rushed to the scenes and gave such acts of charity as they were able. People hugged each other, helped each other, and prayed for each other. People chose to perform acts of kindness, not because God programmed them to do so, but out of their own free will.

Nor did God program the terrorists to carry out their intentions of hatred and evil. The terrorists were fully responsible for what they did. And they will, as will we all, give an account to God for their choices.

How can God be fully in control, yet humans are allowed to make their own choices, even when those choices are destructive, angry, and hateful? It's difficult to reconcile these two major themes of the Bible. Not everything in life can be explained, and life doesn't

always, in fact, make sense. Most of us are pretty logical.
We all know that working out the equation 2 + 2 always
gives us an answer of 4, given the laws of mathematics
in the universe. We expect that life and God similarly
will operate according to a consistent formula.

But they don't.

When disasters happens we often look in vain for a
logical cause-effect relationship that makes sense of
these unforeseen events in our lives or in the lives of
our family members or friends. Only then, we believe,
will we have the information needed to enable us to
move forward. It is disappointing and disheartening
when neither God nor life can be figured out to our
complete satisfaction.

> For the creation was subjected to frustration, not
> by its own choice, but by the will of the one
> who subjected it, in hope that the creation it-
> self will be liberated from its bondage to decay
> and brought into the glorious freedom of the
> children of God.
>
> —Romans 8:20–21

Human beings have choices. As a result of the Fall,
creation as a whole did not have a choice. It was affected by consequences of the actions of Adam. Frustration and decay entered not just the lives of human
beings but into all of the natural order.

Life in neat packages

Frustration, then, is part of the world in which we live, part of every facet of human life. In the interpersonal understanding of what frustration means, we often frustrate other people, including the ones we love the most. Frustration is built into the pattern of every relationship—of every family, school, business, government organization, and church. And this frustration frequently extends to our fallen relationship with God. It means that sometimes we say, "God, it makes no sense."

Those who offer neatly packaged answers to difficult questions and puzzles offer false hope. But even when we can't figure out life or understand the purposes of God, we can still trust that he has a plan and that it is good. We can trust God in the darkness. That also is a choice to do good, a choice to give glory to God.

Those times when life makes the least sense are times during which we grow spiritually. We learn the art of dependence, of how to walk by faith and not by sight. If life always made sense, we would have far less reason to trust God.

But even though there's not always an answer to why disaster happens, God gives a comforting promise for those moments of greatest trauma:

And we know that in all things God works for
the good of those who love him, who have been
called according to his purpose. For those God
foreknew he also predestined to be conformed
to the likeness of his Son, that he might be the
firstborn among many brothers. And those he
predestined, he also called; those he called, he
also justified; those he justified, he also glori-
fied. What, then, shall we say in response to this?
If God is for us, who can be against us? He who
did not spare his own Son, but gave him up for
us all—how will he not also, along with him,
graciously give us all things?

—Romans 8:28–32

Note the question, "If God is for us, who can be
against us?" The implied answer is, "No one!"

Better still, since God is for us, it doesn't matter who's
against us. Even when we experience disaster, God is
still for us. He is always on our side.

Christians do tend to use this text as the panacea
for anyone who is hurting. It was not God's intent
that this promise shut off questioning. He is not here
telling us to "suck it up" and move on. I must confess
that when I stood before the rubble of the fallen Trade
Towers, it was hard to see how God was for us. When
I was diagnosed with probable ALS, it was hard to
accept that God was on my side. My feeling was, "God,

if this is how you are for me, please be for me a little less!"

Paul's foundational point in this Romans passage, which we tend to skip over when we blithely quote it, is that God also has faced the unfairness of sin. He stands beside us as one who knows the pain his wise plan can cause. We are given salvation because Christ faced the most unfair of disasters. In the case of the cross, we can see all the wonders of eternal life opened up because of a horrible disaster. When we begin to see this, we know how good the good is that will result from the "all things" we cannot understand now.

There are moments when we all ask, "How can I be sure that God is on my side?" Paul answers, "He who did not spare his own Son, but gave him up for us all—how will he not also, along with him, graciously give us all things?" The proof that God is for us can be found at the foot of the cross.

In an act of hate, two planes pierced the Trade Towers.

In an act of ultimate love, Christ was pierced for your sin and mine. He was also pierced so that even terrorists (like Saul of Tarsus, who intended to drive all followers of this Jesus into despair and death) might come to him. Jesus died for us all, and the ex-terrorist Saul turned the apostle Paul tells us that, if God gave his Son for us, he will also give to us what we need to deal with the disasters of life.

Living amid the rubble

When you are skeptical about the purpose of God, when it looks as if God has abandoned you, when you're not sure that God is really for you, remember that he has gone through infinite disaster so that you can have victory in the midst of your life disasters. He who did not spare his own Son, but offered him up for us all, will also give us what we need to continue trusting and following him. That may not include answers. We do not really "need" the answers—we only want them, though they would not add to our trust of him if he gave them to us.

God loves me, and in the midst of my doubt and struggle, in the midst of the smoke and rubble, in the midst of the darkness and despair, he has promised to give me what I need to get through it.

The service on that Sunday following the terrorist attacks was like no other in my years as a pastor. Although the sanctuary was packed and people sat on the floor during the services, a somber mood hung about the room. At no time in my life had so many people come to church to hear from God. When disaster strikes, when we are wounded and hurting, there are not simple answers to the questions, "Why, God? Where are you?" But God offers us perspective in his Word. I concluded the sermon that Sunday by giving seven practical responses that every Christian can give from the Bible in light of tragedy:

- *God has not abandoned us.* God is in control, actively involved in the affairs of this world: "In him all things hold together" (Colossians 1:17).
- *God allows fallen and depraved human beings to make their own decisions, even evil ones.* You are free (see Genesis 2:15–17).
- *God doesn't give us all the answers.* We'd like to have all the answers, but we must learn to walk by faith. We can trust God even when life doesn't make sense, even when it seems as if God has abandoned us. "If God is for us, who can be against us?" (Romans 8:31).
- *God will work out all things for his glory.* Good eventually will come out of this tragedy, though we may not know what the good is during this lifetime. "In all things God works for the good of those who love him" (Romans 8:28).
- *God will bring evildoers to justice, whether or not they ever face justice on earth.* All powers were created by and for God, and he is before all things (see Colossians 1:16–17).
- *God will hold us accountable for how we respond to both personal and national disaster.* Just as the terrorists will stand before the Judge of all the earth, so we also will stand before him (see Romans 14:10–12). Evildoers (including terrorists and including us) can be justified through the disaster faced by Christ (Romans 2:9–13; 3:5–24).

- *Disaster and suffering are often used by God to get our attention* (Isaiah 63:9–14; James 1:2–4). As a nation we've put our faith in economic power. But two of our own airplanes, guided by terrorists, reduced the symbol of our economic power to dust. We've put our faith in military might. Another plane, guided by terrorists, greatly damaged the Pentagon—the symbol of our military strength. Could it be that God is trying to get our attention, reminding us that only in him can we safely place our faith?

God certainly got my undivided attention when doctors told me that I likely have ALS. Judging by the dramatic increase in church attendance in the immediate wake of September 11, 2001, God got the attention of millions of Americans and held it long enough that they could see his person.

Where is God, then, when we are driven to our knees and we cry out, "God, where are you?"

His answer is, "I do not change. I'm where I've always been. The question is, 'Where have you been?'"

chapter three

Is God Really in Control?

The LORD reigns, he is robed in majesty;
   the LORD is robed in majesty
   and is armed with strength.
The world is firmly established;
   it cannot be moved.
Your throne was established long ago;
   you are from all eternity.

The seas have lifted up, O LORD,
   the seas have lifted up their voice;
   the seas have lifted up their pounding
   waves.

Mightier than the thunder of the great waters,
   mightier than the breakers of the sea—
   the LORD on high is mighty.

Your statutes stand firm;
   holiness adorns your house
   for endless days, O LORD.

—Psalm 93

CHAPTER 2 INTRODUCED the biblical principle that God is in control. That principle raises two questions:

- Is God responsible for evil?
- Is God directly involved in all tragedies and disasters?

The above psalm begins with three important words: "The LORD reigns." The verb *reigns* is in the present tense. It doesn't say, "There was a time when God reigned." Nor does it say, "There will be a time in the future when God will reign." It says that God is reigning right now.

This proclamation is not conditioned upon certain circumstances or situations. It is an absolute declaration that our God is now reigning.

This statement is actually part of a formula. Whenever a new king was anointed in Israel, the people would proclaim, "So-and-so is king!" This declaration was spread throughout the land, passed from person to person, community to community, village to village. The psalmist begins this powerful psalm by making a similar declaration about God. It, too, is meant to be passed from person to person, community to community, and village to village: "The LORD reigns!"

Say it to yourself again and again. "The LORD reigns."

When disaster comes, declare in the face of it, "The LORD reigns."

When towers fall, respond with this proclamation: "The LORD reigns!"

Our confidence is that, no matter what, God is in control.

If God really reigns, then is he responsible for the falling World Trade Center Towers? If God reigns, why does tragedy come into our lives? What does it mean that God reigns or is in control?

In theological terms, the control of the Lord over all that happens is described as the *sovereignty* of God, which is the quality of God's being supreme, unchallenged, above everyone and everything. The supremacy of God is a major theme of the Bible, and God's supremacy encompasses rank, authority, and purpose.

God is supreme in rank. God is above every conceivable hierarchy. Whether political, religious, legal, or any other institutional power, God is above it all. He is the highest in rank.

Clap your hands, all you nations;
    shout to God with cries of joy.
How awesome is the LORD Most High,
    the great King over all the earth!
                                —Psalm 47:1-2

All the gods of this world combined and the power that they claim cannot compare to the one true God. God is the "great King over all the earth," greater than all the political kingdoms of this world and all the political leaders combined.

God is supreme in authority. God's authority is supreme and unchallenged among all conceivable powers and authorities:

> The LORD has established his throne in heaven,
> and his kingdom rules over all.
> —Psalm 103:19

Note that God's authority extends over all the earth and is not limited to certain places or peoples. His is a supreme authority that extends over all.

God is supreme in his purpose.

> By the word of the LORD were the heavens made,
> their starry host by the breath of his mouth.
> He gathers the waters of the sea into jars;
> he puts the deep into storehouses.

> Let all the earth fear the LORD;
> let all the people of the world revere him.
> For he spoke, and it came to be;
> he commanded, and it stood firm.
> The LORD foils the plans of the nations;

he thwarts the purposes of the peoples.
But the plans of the LORD stand firm forever,
the purposes of his heart through all
generations.

—Psalm 33:6–11

The plans of the Lord—his purposes—"stand firm forever." And God always accomplishes what he sets out to do. He even "foils" and "thwarts" the plans of other peoples and nations.

Sovereignty and chaos

Have you faced a time when everything seemed unstable and unpredictable? Have you ever felt that your life was out of control, in a downward spiral that you couldn't stop? In such times consider Psalm 93, with which this chapter opened: "The LORD reigns, he is robed in majesty; the LORD is robed in majesty and is armed with strength" (Psalm 93:1a). At this point in the biblical text, a *therefore* should be inserted to introduce the logical conclusion of the first statement about God: *Therefore* "the world is firmly established; it cannot be moved" (v. 1b).

Psalm 93 continues, "Your throne was established long ago; you are from all eternity" (v. 2). So even if your life, your very world, seems out of control, know the great truth of Scripture—God is in control.

Certainly, the events of September 11 changed America forever, but God has not changed. He was the same on September 10, on September 11, and on September 12—the same as he is today and as he will be tomorrow and forever. His throne and his authority, his supremacy and his will, his purposes and his counsel are forever settled in heaven and on the earth.

God is sovereign. Hallelujah.

One can make a powerful argument for the sovereignty of God when things are neat and orderly. But what about when things are in utter chaos? The sovereignty of God sounds good in a theology class or a Sunday sermon, but what about when one is standing before the rubble of the Trade Towers? In the light of such uncontrollable circumstances how can we still make the claim, "God is in control"?

The psalmist addresses this question:

> The seas have lifted up, O LORD,
>   the seas have lifted up their voice;
>   the seas have lifted up their pounding waves.
> Mightier than the thunder of the great waters,
>   mightier than the breakers of the sea—
>   the LORD on high is mighty.
>   —Psalm 93:3–4

These words are most meaningful to those who have watched the ocean attacking the shore or a ship during a terrific storm. The pounding of the waves against the rocks offers a picture of immense power. This psalm likens the image of a raging sea to the chaos of creation. And even when creation is in chaos, lifting up its voice against God, God is still enthroned supreme and unchallenged. The utter chaos that is all around has no might that is able to challenge his throne.

But if we believe that God is reigning to the extent that the Bible says he is, then we must assume that he either forgot to reign on September 11, 2001, or else he turned his back on us. Assuming an infinitely powerful God leaves us with two possible extremes.

The first position is what I call "rocking chair theology."

Some people suggest that God created the world, ruled the world, and established the moral, natural, and spiritual laws that govern the world. But once he had set the world in motion, he decided to sit back in a rocking chair to watch what would happen. In this scenario, he is not now actively involved in the running of the world. Rather, he is allowing the world to take its course.

If we follow this line of thinking to its logical conclusion, the answer to "Where was God on September 11?" is simple. He wasn't there at all, because disaster is completely irrelevant to God. This position makes it easier to defend God's integrity in relation to evil when disasters happen. Unfortunately, it also reduces God to a meaningless and uncaring sky deity. This is the sort of deity worshiped by the ancient pagans, not the sort defined in Scripture. If God is removed from the day-to-day struggles of humanity, why bother praying to him? Why read the Bible? Why serve and love him?

The position at the other extreme suggests that God is involved in every detail of life. It assumes that God predetermines every single event in human history and in our lives. God then becomes the master puppeteer and we become the puppets on his strings. If this is true, then God was directly involved on September 11 and in every disaster that comes your way and my way. God has the right, of course, to rule this way if he so chooses. He is, after all, the creator, and as such maintains the right to do as he pleases.

But this concept of God—a God who makes bad things happen—is rather frightening. But these two positions—God as completely removed from disaster and God as the direct cause of disaster—fall far short of the actual role of God as described in Scripture. Remember the foundational truth: God reigns. In fact, he reigns at three different levels.

God of the big picture

God reigns in a general sense over all creation.

> For by him all things were created: things in heaven and on earth, visible and invisible,

whether thrones or powers or rulers or authorities; all things were created by him and for him.
He is before all things, and in him all things
hold together.

—Colossians 1:16–17

Two levels of God's reign are contained in this passage: First, he rules in creation because he is its author
and finisher. Through Jesus, God brought the universe
into existence. Second, God rules in creation through
Jesus. Jesus holds the entire world together.

Given the intricate balance of natural forces that allow
life to exist on this planet—including the precise rotation
and orbit of the sun necessary for our existence—what
would happen to life on earth if Jesus took his hand off
the universe for even a moment? If there is chaos now,
what indeed would the universe look like without a
ruler?

Without Jesus holding the universe together we'd be
in serious trouble. We wouldn't want to live in a world
where Jesus was not directly involved.

God is working his ultimate purpose for all of creation.

And he made known to us the mystery of his
will according to his good pleasure, which he
purposed in Christ, to be put into effect when
the times will have reached their fulfillment—

> to bring all things in heaven and on earth to-
> gether under one head, even Christ.
>
> —Ephesians 1:9–10

At a third level we see that God has a final purpose for all of creation and is actively engaged in accomplishing this purpose. That ultimate purpose is to bring all creation under the lordship of Jesus Christ. In the midst of chaos, when people ask, "Where is it all going?" the answer is simple: God is working out his will and purpose on the earth, moving history toward the day when all of creation will be under one head—even Jesus. Consider, then, the three levels at which God rules in this world:

> God created the world.
> Jesus holds the world together.
> God is at work, moving toward his ultimate purpose.

God is not, then, an absentee landlord for creation, sitting in a rocking chair hoping eternity will somehow work itself out. He is the ruler of the universe.

All is not well, though, on planet earth. It is broken, an imperfect world filled with imperfect people. And while God rules in a general sense over all creation, his rule is opposed at every step by another ruler—Satan, the "ruler of the kingdom of the air" (Ephesians 2:2). While God moves history to its ultimate purpose, another kingdom is at work—the kingdom of Satan.

We humans live between the tensions of these two kingdoms in conflict.

> As for you, you were dead in your transgressions and sins, in which you used to live when you followed the ways of this world and of the ruler of the kingdom of the air, the spirit who is now at work in those who are disobedient.
>
> —Ephesians 2:1–2

Satan is alive and well on earth, and the evil he promotes is all around us—in individual lives, families, and institutions. When it appears that evil triumphs more often than good, how can we say that God rules?

A threefold relationship exists between God's rule and evil.

First, God permits evil. God created a perfect world, devoid of the presence of evil. But God did not create a world devoid of the *potential* for evil. He created human beings, as well as Satan, with the ability to make choices. God told Adam and Eve, "You are free to eat from any tree in the garden; but you must not eat from the tree of the knowledge of good and evil, for when you eat of it you will surely die"(Genesis 2:16–17). Notice the key words *free to eat.* Humans were created with the potential to sin or not to sin. Choice is a gift from the Creator, but God does not predetermine what humans will do.

The same was true with Satan, who at one time was a beautiful angel but chose to rebel against God. God permits people—and angels—to make their own choices, even when those choices are destructive to others. The terrorists who flew into the Trade Towers, the Pentagon, and a Pennsylvania field acted of their own free wills.

Second, God restrains sin and evil: "For the secret power of lawlessness is already at work; but the one who now holds it back will continue to do so till he is taken out of the way" (2 Thessalonians 2:7). This text from Thessalonians reminds us that the power of lawlessness is active on earth; we see it all around us. But God's permission of evil does not mean that he is helpless in the face of it. God actively holds evil back, and without his restraint, evil would be far worse than it is. Even Satan lives within the boundaries that God establishes. Satan tormented God's servant Job only to the degree that God allowed (Job 2:6).

Third, God redeems evil. God's allowing evil and restraining evil are defensive in nature. Thus, the third dimension of his relationship to evil is proactive—God redeems evil for his purpose. Joseph discovered this principle after his jealous brothers sold him into slavery. Joseph eventually acquired an elevated position in Egypt, where, years later, his brothers came to buy grain. When they discovered that Joseph had become second in command to Pharaoh, the brothers feared for their lives. Joseph had every reason to get even with them. But Joseph understood that God transforms evil for his glory and purposes. He reassured his brothers that he would not harm them:

> Don't be afraid. Am I in the place of God? You intended to harm me, but God intended it for good to accomplish what is now being done, the saving of many lives.
>
> —Genesis 50:19–20

While God rules in general over creation, he rules in specifics in the church, where his rule should be uncontested.

> And he is the head of the body, the church; he is the beginning and the firstborn from among the dead, so that in everything he might have the supremacy.
>
> —Colossians 1:18

Jesus is the head of the body, which is the church. Thus, God is to be preeminent in the lives of his people and in the embassy mission of the church. Unbelievers should be able to witness the rule of God by looking at us, the members of the body who are the church. Thus, we are to demonstrate the reign of God to those around us by showing his character to a world in chaos. In the midst of the darkness of this world, God has placed his kingdom communities of light. When we speak of the holiness of God, we are to reflect that holiness in our lives. When we speak of the love of God, we are to reflect that love. When we speak of the justice of God, we are to reflect that justice.

The final focal point of disaster

When disaster comes—and it will come—our response is to demonstrate the hope, love, forgiveness, justice, holiness, and patience of the God we serve.

While God rules specifically over his people, one day he will rule absolutely over all people.

> The kingdom of the world has become the kingdom of our Lord and of his Christ, and he will reign for ever and ever.
>
> —Revelation 11:15b

This verse states our hope: Satan will be judged and condemned, creation will be liberated from its decay and bondage. There will be no more disasters or suffering; no more cancer, ALS, MS, or any other kind of sickness and disease. There will be no more hatred and evil. The old way of living will pass away and in that day God will make everything new.

When our world seems out of control and disaster comes our way, we can be confident that God has not abandoned us. He is still at work, moving all of creation toward his larger purpose—bringing it under the lordship of the Son, Jesus.

> The LORD reigns, he is robed in majesty;
>   the LORD is robed in majesty
>   and is armed with strength.
> The world is firmly established;
>   it cannot be moved.
>   —Psalm 93:1

In the world as we know it and live in it, God allows evil to exist. He allows us as humans to make our own decisions even when those decisions are against his moral will as defined in Scripture, even when they are destructive and hateful. But God is not helpless against evil. He restrains it and transforms it into something good. When towers fall, God builds something beautiful out of the ruins. When suffering invades my life as an unwelcome guest, God turns it into something good.

How should we face disaster in light of these truths?

First, focus on God. It is much easier to focus on disaster and suffering than to focus on God. If my focus is on my struggle, then I will most often walk in fear. But if I focus on God—who reigns over all of creation, who rules directly over the church, who will one day rule absolutely over all the universe—then I can rest assured that he is in control.

Second, when dealing with disaster, remember three things:

1. Remember that God uses disaster to demonstrate how the people of God deal with the difficulties of life.
2. Remember that we are living illustrations of what the rule of God looks like on earth. How we respond to disaster can attract people to the God who is in control, or it can drive them further away from him.
3. Remember—always—that the Lord reigns!

chapter four

Is It the End of the World?

Oh, that you would rend the heavens and
   come down,
that the mountains would tremble before
   you!
As when fire sets twigs ablaze
   and causes water to boil,
come down to make your name known to
   your enemies
   and cause the nations to quake before you!

For when you did awesome things that we did
   not expect,
you came down, and the mountains trembled
   before you.
Since ancient times no one has heard,
   no ear has perceived,
no eye has seen any God besides you,

who acts on behalf of those who wait for him.
You come to the help of those who gladly do
     right,
     who remember your ways.
But when we continued to sin against them,
     you were angry.

     How then can we be saved?
All of us have become like one who is
     unclean,
     and all our righteous acts are like filthy rags;
we all shrivel up like a leaf,
     and like the wind our sins sweep us away.

No one calls on your name
     or strives to lay hold of you;
for you have hidden your face from us
     and made us waste away because of our
     sins.

Yet, O LORD, you are our Father.
     We are the clay, you are the potter;
     we are all the work of your hand.
Do not be angry beyond measure, O LORD;
     do not remember our sins forever.
Oh, look upon us, we pray,
     for we are all your people.

                              —Isaiah 64:1–9

WHENEVER MAJOR CRISIS events occur, people speculate that it might be a sign—perhaps a sign that the Lord is coming immediately and that the end of the world is near.

During the Second World War, a great many people were convinced that Adolf Hitler was the Antichrist and that he was trying to unite Europe, just as the Bible predicted.

During previous conflicts in the Middle East and the more recent Gulf War, sales on prophecy books soared. War was being waged in the Middle East, Israel was being attacked with missiles, and many of the armies of the world were gathered to fight.

As we approached the end of the twentieth century, speculation rose that we were coming to the end of the world as we know it. Many predicted that Jesus would come before the end of 1999.

When the Trade Towers and the Pentagon were hit, people asked if this was a sign of the end of the world. A survey of high school students in our church the week after the attacks revealed that more than one-third of their questions concerned the end of the world: Do the events of September 11 indicate that we are moving closer to the end? Are these occurrences part of the biblical prophecies about the coming of the Lord and the end of the world?

To answer these questions, we must look at the biblical prophecies about the end times and then determine if they relate to the most recent terrorist attacks on America. In the Olivet Discourse, found in Matthew 24 and 25, Jesus speaks of signs that indicate the approaching end of the world. His disciples come to him and ask, "Tell us, when will this happen, and what will be the sign of your coming and of the end of the age?"(24:3b). Jesus responds with a description of circumstances on earth before he returns and the end comes. Among the signs mentioned in Matthew 24 are the following.

Wars and rumors of wars

As we approach the end, circumstances on earth will not get better. In fact, they will get worse. Jesus said, "Nation will rise against nation, and kingdom against kingdom" (Matthew 24:7a). While people will seek peace, they will experience only war. Evidence of this is as close as tomorrow's newspaper.

As an example, Al-Qaida, the group given most responsibility for the September 11 attacks, comprises seven violent terrorist organizations. Al-Qaida is one of about a dozen major Islamic organizations dedicated to establishing regional or world jihad (holy war). Islamic fundamentalism represents one of the most vocal and visible movements dedicated to throwing the world into a bloodbath of chaos. But look at what modern weaponry has contributed to ancient tribal conflicts in Africa. Look at the unrest in Central and South America; in the Balkans; in Irish and Scottish nationalism.

Famines

Jesus predicted the coming of famines, as do other Bible passages that refer to the Tribulation (Revelation 6:6). Scientists are concerned about the growth of world population and humanity's inability to grow enough food for itself. Thus, global famine is a realistic possibility.

Earthquakes

Most students of prophecy claim that in recent years the number of earthquakes has increased. This is not true, however, according to the National Earthquake Information Center, which says that the number of earthquakes of 7.0 magnitude or greater remained constant through the twentieth century. But earthquakes do continue and they will increase as we approach the end of the world.

Persecution of Christians

The world always has hated Christians—even as they hated Jesus. But as the spirit of the age becomes increasingly that of the Antichrist, the persecution of

Christians will increase. Christians will be martyred for their faith—a trend that reached an unprecedented level around the world during the twentieth century.

Increased wickedness

As the end approaches, so will the increase of wickedness and sin. Paul also speaks of these days, describing them as "terrible":

> People will be lovers of themselves, lovers of money, boastful, proud, abusive, disobedient to their parents, ungrateful, unholy, without love, unforgiving, slanderous, without self-control, brutal, not lovers of the good, treacherous, rash, conceited, lovers of pleasure rather than lovers of God.
>
> —2 Timothy 3:2–4

The terrorist acts committed against the innocent people in the Towers surely fit Paul's description. Words like *brutal, treacherous,* and *rash* certainly capture the horrific nature of these attacks.

False messiahs

Jesus predicted that many would come in his name, claiming to be the Christ, or Messiah. Other Bible passages, too (2 Corinthians 11:13–14; 2 Peter 2:1–3), confirm that there will be a proliferation of false messiahs before the last days. Certainly there has never been a lack of charismatic individuals who have stirred messianic fervor. Since the Russian Revolution, mass media has given both national and international leaders an unheralded forum for exciting the populace with their promises.

Further signs of the end of the world appear in both the Old and New Testaments. Merging the predictions in general categories gives a clear picture of what the world will look like before the second coming of the Lord.

Political predictions

The focus of international attention in the end time will be on Israel. The Bible predicts the regathering of the Jews back to their homeland, with the city of Jerusalem under Jewish control. Israel and its neighbors will experience ongoing hostility despite many attempts to broker peace agreements.

The Bible also predicts a revival of the ancient Roman Empire that will produce an economic and military coalition across Europe.

A major shift to globalism will lead to a one-world economy and government. Along with these political and military developments will be an increase in international instability.

Technological predictions

God predicted an increase in knowledge at the approach of the end of the age. We now live along the information superhighway, and knowledge has increased exponentially in our generation.

There also will be a shift to a cashless society. Computers and microchips could be a technological herald to Revelation's mark of the Beast, which will be necessary for the buying and selling of goods.

Religious predictions

The Bible predicts that the temple in Jerusalem will be rebuilt in the last days. A shift toward a one-world religion will occur. Although the Bible does not mention Islam, it does predict that a coalition of nations will invade Israel with the intention of driving them into the sea. Many scholars believe that this coalition will consist of the Muslim and Arab nations that surround Israel.

Aside from the preceding predictions, the next significant event in human history is the rapture of the church, the first event that is related directly to the Second Coming of the Lord. Christ will come to call all believers home to heaven. The dead will rise first, and then those who are alive will be caught up with them to meet the Lord in the air (1 Thessalonians 4:15–17).

Following the Rapture, a period of seven years called the Great Tribulation, will transpire. During this period, the Antichrist will emerge, and the entire world will come under his political influence. He will negotiate peace in the troubled parts of the world, including the Middle East. In due time, he will turn against the Jews and persecute them.

The Tribulation will end with the Battle of Armageddon, when the armies of the world will gather against Israel. At the last moment Christ will return with the armies of heaven and defeat the forces that are aligned against Israel. Then Jesus will establish his millennial kingdom and reign physically for one thousand years.

While Christians have always believed that Jesus could come at any time, those who have speculated that they were living in the last days have always been wrong.

> So when they met together, they asked him, "Lord, are you at this time going to restore the kingdom to Israel?" He said to them: "It is not for you to know the times or dates the Father has set by his own authority."
>
> —Acts 1:6–7

> No one knows about that day or hour, not even the angels in heaven, nor the Son, but only the Father.
>
> —Matthew 24:36

While the Bible gives many predictions, some detailed, about the coming of the Lord and the end of the world, no one—except the Father—knows when this precise sequence of events will actually occur. Anyone who claims knowledge of a specific time must, therefore, know more than the angels and Jesus himself. It is true that many things in the current world situation certainly parallel the events predicted in the Bible, but one must be careful not to speculate that we are living in the last days. We may be, and we may not be. Jesus could come at any moment, but he may tarry for another thousand years or longer. It's all up to the Father.

Now we have the basis on which to answer those who wonder about a connection between September 11 and the coming of Jesus and the end of the world. In a broad sense, there is a connection. We know that *all* things in this world are moving toward the coming of the Lord and the end of the world. All events of human history are, therefore, heading toward the greater purpose of God, which is to bring all things under the headship of his Son, Jesus. The events of September 11 do not, however, signal fulfillment of any specific prophecy that would indicate that the coming of the Lord is upon us.

One could speculate about the political and military circumstances that have resulted from the attacks. What if the coalition of Arab and Muslim nations that supports us now were to turn against us and evolve into a world Islamic alliance to deal with Israel? What if they formed a broad Muslim coalition to fight the West and the nation of Israel? What if Jewish religious fanatics blow up the Dome of the Rock in order to clear the ground for a rebuilt temple?

What if . . . ?

What if . . . ?

What if . . . ?

It is my opinion that no direct connection can be drawn from the events of September 11 to the prophecies about the coming of the Lord and the end of the world.

Being prepared

This chapter began with Jesus' teachings about the end of the world. Although Christ was not specific about a sequence of events or a particular time frame for when these events would be set in motion, he does not leave us without guidance regarding how to prepare for the last times. His sermon ends with practical advice about how we are to live in light of his coming and the approaching end of the world.

He concludes his counsel with three stories.

The first is the parable of the ten virgins who are waiting long hours for the bridegroom to come and start the wedding feast. This story presents an obvious instruction about how to be prepared for the coming of the Lord. The story, told in Matthew 25:1–13, relates that each of the women had a lamp, basically a small pot filled with oil, from which a small wick extended. The oil in these lamps could burn quickly, and the bridegroom in Jesus' story had not arrived, though it was long after dark. Five of the women had anticipated that this might happen, so they had brought extra oil to refill their lamps. Jesus called these five women wise because they had considered contingencies and were prepared and willing to wait, no matter how long.

He called the other five women foolish because they did not bring extra oil. When the bridegroom was delayed, the women all became drowsy and fell asleep. By the time they awakened, all the lamps needed more oil. But the ones who did not prepare had none. They needed to buy more oil, but while they were away, the bridegroom arrived. The five foolish women missed the feast.

Jesus concluded the story with this warning: "Therefore keep watch, because you do not know the day or the hour" (v. 13). The message is clear: First, we do not know when Jesus will come. It could be today or tomorrow or it might still lie centuries into the future. Second, we should be ready for his coming at any moment. We don't want to be like the foolish virgins who were not prepared for the coming of the bridegroom.

And how are we to prepare? Jesus tells us in the next two parables.

The second parable, told in Matthew 25:14–30, is that of the ten talents, a lesson about being good stewards of what God has given. A talent was a unit of weight by which large amounts of gold or silver were counted. Jesus tells the story of a rich landowner who went on a journey and entrusted his property to three of his servants. He gave the first man five talents—a significant amount of money. To the second man he gave two talents, and to the third, one talent, which was still a considerable wealth. During the owner's absence the man with five talents worked hard and doubled the investment, gaining another five talents. The man with two talents also worked hard and also earned one hundred percent profit on the investment, gaining two more. But the man with one talent dug a hole in the ground and hid the money.

When the property owner returned, he met with the three men for an accounting of their efforts. He was pleased with the first two and commended them both. "Well done, good and faithful servant! You have been faithful with a few things; I will put you in charge of many things. Come and share your master's happiness!" (Matthew 25:21, 23). But the owner was not at all pleased with the third man, who had nothing more to show for the investment than what the owner gave him. The last man had done nothing with his talent, and the owner called him a "wicked, lazy servant" (v. 26). He took the talent and gave it to the first man, then threw the lazy servant out into the darkness.

The truth revealed in this story is that God has given each of us assets—time, money, abilities, and other mercies by his hand that he wants us to put to use to further his kingdom. One day when Jesus returns, he will judge our stewardship of the resources he has given us. It is our responsibility to invest all that we are and have in strategic ways to advance the interests of the Master—God. If we are faithful stewards of these resources, we will be commended and put in charge of more in the earthly kingdom of Christ.

The third parable, Matthew 25:31–46, is of the sheep and the goats, a tale that relates how true faith is authenticated in compassion for the poor. The parable concerns the day of judgment when Jesus comes to separate the sheep (his followers) from the goats (nonbelievers). The focus of the parable is on the criteria by which Jesus will make his judgments. People will be measured by what they did for the hungry, the thirsty, the homeless, the naked, the sick, and those in prison (vv. 34–36). Those who have true life in Christ and express this life in love will be invited into the kingdom; those who have no life and no love to share will be "cursed" and thrown into "eternal fire prepared for the devil and his angels" (v. 41).

This is a disturbing story. Jesus certainly is not saying that our efforts on behalf of the poor and disenfranchised will earn us a ticket to heaven. Rather, he is saying that our salvation by grace will respond to need naturally. The major truth is both mysterious and discomforting: When we minister to the poor, we are ministering to Jesus. When Jesus judges the goats, the nonbelievers, he declares, "I was hungry and you gave me nothing to eat, I was thirsty and you gave me nothing to drink, I was a stranger and you did not invite me in, I needed clothes and you did not clothe me, I was sick and in prison and you did not look after me" (vv. 42–43). Those receiving this rebuke are shocked: "We never saw you that way," they said. Their implication is that, had they seen Jesus with any of these needs, they would have immediately responded.

Jesus declares that they did, indeed, see him because he was identified with the poor. When they ignored human need around them they had really rejected him directly: "I tell you the truth, whatever you did not do for one of the least of these, you did not do for me" (v. 45).

When we give food to the hungry, we are giving it to the Lord himself. Likewise, when we give water to the thirsty, when we shelter the homeless and clothe the naked, we are caring for the needs of Jesus. When we visit the sick and prisoners, we are visiting Jesus. To touch them and care for their needs is to touch and care for the needs of Jesus. Note that this advice concludes Jesus' sermon on the end of the world and how we should prepare for it.

In the face of all this broken world's tragedies and in light of the coming of the Lord, how, then, should we live? Jesus gives a clear answer. We should be ready—because we do not know when he will return. We should invest the resources and gifts that God has given us—because to do so is to advance his gospel in the world. We should reach out to and touch the hurting people who are in desperate need in our own communities—because when we touch them, we are touching Jesus himself.

chapter five

WHAT ABOUT EVIL?

Judge me, O LORD, according to my
   righteousness,
      according to my integrity, O Most High.
O righteous God,
   who searches minds and hearts,
bring to an end the violence of the wicked
   and make the righteous secure.
My shield is God Most High,
   who saves the upright in heart.

God is a righteous judge,
   a God who expresses his wrath every day.
If he does not relent,
   he will sharpen his sword;
      he will bend and string his bow.
He has prepared his deadly weapons;
   he makes ready his flaming arrows.

He who is pregnant with evil
and conceives trouble gives birth to
disillusionment.
He who digs a hole and scoops it out
falls into the pit he has made.
The trouble he causes recoils on himself;
his violence comes down on his own head.

I will give thanks to the LORD because of his
righteousness
and will sing praise to the name of the LORD
Most High.

—Psalm 7:8b–17

A FEW WEEKS AFTER the World Trade Center Towers fell, I facilitated a meeting of about fifteen business and educational leaders from our city. We met for several hours to talk about the impact of the events of September 11 on people's lives within the community and on the organizations that were represented. It was not a faith-based group, and most of the people who attended were not known for their professions of a solid devotion to Jesus. Essentially their perspectives and the resulting discussion revolved around secular wisdom. At one point, one distinguished physician and scientist tendered his opinion: "I don't believe there is such a thing as evil—only a lack of love."

Under other circumstances, the statement might have

resonated with at least a few others in the group. But in the context of recent events, no one seemed to know what to say in response. How could anyone possibly think that evil does not exist in the face of twenty-three acres of rubble and the loss of thousands of innocent lives?

Yet there was an element of truth in what he said. If every person loved God and his or her neighbor, the world would, indeed, be different. But loving God and neighbor are not universal human characteristics. Something far less desirable takes their place in human relations.

During times of disaster, nearly everyone believes in some sort of evil principle, something that might be vaguely called a "devil." The question of what sort of devil may be at work would raise more differences of opinion. For many, the Devil is a cartoon character dressed in a bright red suit, carrying a pitchfork. Rather than a being who strikes fear in the hearts of humans, the Devil is a fantasy imp whose wickedness amounts to little more than stirring up a bit of mischief. He's good for a practical joke or a derisive laugh—nothing more.

But this is not what the Bible says about the Devil. The Devil is one of the leading causes of trouble and evil in the world.

The Bible uses a variety of names for the Devil:

- He's called *Satan*, which means "adversary."
- He's called the *Devil*, which means "slanderer."
- He's called the *Serpent*, which describes his craftiness.
- He's called the *Dragon* and a *roaring lion*, which describes his power.
- He's called a *tempter* and an *angel of light* to recognize his subtle persuasions.
- He's called the *ruler of this world* and *Beelzebub* (lord or chief among the flies or demons) to signify something of his spheres of authority.

Satan is alive and well

All such titles and descriptive names reveal the character of Satan, as well as his purposes. His primary objective is to oppose God and God's purposes. Satan tempted Adam and Eve in the Garden of Eden until they rebelled against God, an action that plunged the whole human race into death. Satan tempted Jesus in the wilderness but could not succeed against God's holy and undefiled Son. Satan blinds the minds of unbelievers so that they will not respond to the gospel, and on a geopolitical scale he works constantly at deceiving the nations.

Need one wonder why there is so much evil in the world? Satan is alive and well, and he and the other demons are working against the purposes of God. So when towers fall and innocent lives are lost, we should be shocked—but not surprised. Satan causes chaos and disruption, working day and night to oppose God, to turn the world away from God and to himself.

Satan was created as a mighty angel, but he rebelled and fell from heaven:

> How you have fallen from heaven,
>   O morning star, son of the dawn!
> You have been cast down to the earth,
>   you who once laid low the nations!
> You said in your heart,
>   "I will ascend to heaven;
> I will raise my throne above the stars of God;
> I will sit enthroned on the mount of the
>   assembly,
> on the utmost heights of the sacred
>   mountain.
> I will ascend above the tops of the clouds;
>   I will make myself like the Most High."
> But you are brought down to the grave,
>   to the depths of the pit.
>   —Isaiah 14:12–15

Satan still tries to elevate himself above God, and he still wreaks havoc in the world. And Satan is not alone in his program to oppose God. Not omnipresent as is God, Satan is limited to being in one place at a time.

But he is accompanied by legions of demons, angels who followed Satan when he fell from heaven. Satan's demons inhabit the world and help him carry out his diabolical plans.

One of the responsibilities of demons regards the affairs of nations. In the book of Daniel, Daniel has a vision of an angel coming to him from God. When the angel arrives he reveals some startling news about his journey:

> "Do not be afraid, Daniel. Since the first day that you set your mind to gain understanding and to humble yourself before your God, your words were heard, and I have come in response to them. But the prince of the Persian kingdom resisted me twenty-one days. Then Michael, one of the chief princes, came to help me, because I was detained there with the king of Persia."
>
> —Daniel 10:12–13

This passage suggests that an evil angel responsible for the Persian kingdom delayed the angel sent from God. He was so powerful that the efforts of another good angel, Michael, were required to defeat the wicked angel. This passage suggests that demons are assigned to nations and exercise influence over them, opposing the work of God in regard to those nations.

The seed of opposition

It's not difficult to understand why so much conflict confounds the nations. And where is the seed of conflict sown? In the hearts and minds of human beings. God has placed human beings in this world, in which Satan and his demons are alive and well, doing all that lies within their power to oppose the work of God. And like the world around us, we are broken, as Paul describes in the epistle to the Romans in a collection of biblical quotations about the problem facing humanity.

> "There is no one righteous, not even one;
>   there is no one who understands,
>   no one who seeks God.
> All have turned away,
>   they have become worthless;
> there is no one who does good,
>   not even one."
> "Their throats are open graves;
>   their tongues practice deceit."
> "The poison of vipers is on their lips."
>   "Their mouths are full of cursing and bitterness."
> "Their feet are swift to shed blood;
>   ruin and misery mark their ways,
> and the way of peace they do not know."
>   "There is no fear of God before their eyes."
> —Romans 3:10–18

These are ugly descriptions that may bring to mind some individuals we know. But before we fill in the blanks of these descriptions with the names of others—perhaps the terrorists who destroyed the Trade Center Towers—we should remember that the apostle Paul applies them to *us*. We are all sinners. We all have fallen short of God's standard.

We are quick to see the evil in the brutal act of the terrorists, but very slow to see the evil that is at work in our own lives. We condemn Osama bin Laden and the Al-Qaida network of terrorists, declaring rather presumptuously that we will stamp out such evil anywhere it might be found in the world. But we fail to see the vestiges of terrorism against God that we ourselves shelter. We rebel against the will of God for our lives, misusing our free will, abusing our spouses and children, and wrecking the lives of those who love us.

As long as we can focus on the evil of others, we can avoid looking at the evil in our own minds.

In reality, we all are capable of acts of unspeakable terror because fallen human beings are by nature depraved and in need of the forgiveness and redemption of God. What the terrorists did is a great evil. But in light of the presence of Satan and his demons in the world, in light of the fallen state of humanity, can we not understand why such evil occurs? The terrorists, like us, are sinners. For all of us, separated from God and left on our own, there are no limits to the evil we are capable of perpetrating.

Further, the evil we as individuals cause and experience is felt in all of creation itself:

> I consider that our present sufferings are not worth comparing with the glory that will be revealed in us. The creation waits in eager expectation for the sons of God to be revealed. For the creation was subjected to frustration, not by its own choice, but by the will of the one who subjected it, in hope that the creation itself will be liberated from its bondage to decay and brought into the glorious freedom of the children of God.
>
> —Romans 8:18–21

The Bible tells us that frustration is the state of all existence. None of our human institutions—families, schools, churches, governments—is perfect. The best families are flawed, as are the best schools, the best churches, the best governments. All function with sins, moral weaknesses, and hidden agendas that cause frustration in all who come into contact with them. This is the harsh reality of life on earth.

Consider, for instance, the quest for peace in the Middle East. For decades, the United States has been one of the countries most intensely involved in brokering a peace accord among Palestinians, other Muslim peoples, and the Jews. For every step forward, however, the effort has taken ten steps backward toward the edge of an abyss. The results have been frustration—exactly as the Bible states. In many respects, Middle East peace seems no closer now than it did decades ago. While efforts at a peace agreement should continue in the various Middle East conflicts, we must accept the reality that those efforts will be frustrating at best.

Broken people in a broken world

The Bible makes it clear that we are broken people living in a broken world. Still, most of the world was shocked at the nature and extent of the violence of recent terrorism, and especially the attacks in New York and Washington, D.C. Those events are incomprehensible. September 11, 2001, forced governments around the world to face the harsh realities about evil and its devastating results.

But those realities should not be a complete surprise to those who believe the Bible. The institutions in which we live and work are filled with frustration and decay. The people with which we interact are—like us—sinners, and as such are capable of the terrible acts that seem unimaginable in civilized society. With Satan and his demons tempting humans to sin and opposing the plan of God for the world, nothing that happens in this world should surprise us by the depths of its depravity.

While the preceding analysis may shed light on the subject of evil, it doesn't offer much hope to those who are frustrated. It may help explain evil but it doesn't give us a way out.

But there *is* a way out. The God who allows Satan, his demons, and humans to make their own choices in a frustrating world—that God sent his only Son into this world in order to redeem fallen humans and ultimately to restore the world to its original perfect condition:

> For God so loved the world that he gave his one and only Son, that whoever believes in him shall not perish but have eternal life. For God did not send his Son into the world to condemn the world, but to save the world through him.
> —John 3:16–17

God loves the world. He loves you and me—and he loves terrorists who plot to fly planes into buildings. He proved his love by sending his only Son into the world. When Jesus died on the cross, God took my sins, your sins, the sins of the terrorists, of Osama bin Laden, of the whole world, and placed all those sins on Jesus Christ. Jesus suffered, shed his blood, and rose again as our substitute. We deserved to suffer and die but Jesus took our place. Anyone who believes in Jesus will not perish but will receive everlasting life.

This is the gospel, the Good News. It is the only message that tells us how we can be restored to God and to each other across ethnic, tribal, economic, and religious divisions.

In the face of September 11, in the face of terrible evil, we have good news for a world mired in futility, desperation, and frustration. It is the gospel of forgiveness and reconciliation. It is the only message that can bring peace to a troubled world; and to an extent unknown for decades, people have listened to its message.

It is a message that reconciles us to God and to each other across racial, ethnic, and religious divides.

chapter six

WHO IS TO BLAME WHEN
TOWERS FALL?

Now there were some present at that time who
told Jesus about the Galileans whose blood
Pilate had mixed with their sacrifices. Jesus answered, "Do you think that these Galileans were
worse sinners than all the other Galileans because they suffered this way? I tell you, no! But
unless you repent, you too will all perish. Or
those eighteen who died when the tower of
Siloam fell on them—do you think they were
more guilty than all the others living in Jerusalem? I tell you, no! But unless you repent, you
too will all perish."

—Luke 13:1–5

WHO IS TO BLAME when disaster comes? Some Christian
leaders stirred controversy when they blamed the falling
Trade Center Towers on the increasing secularization

of America. These analysts have speculated that America historically has enjoyed the divine protection of God because we were a "Christian nation." But over recent decades, we have drifted far from our religious roots, and God now has lifted his protection, allowing the terrible events of September 11, 2001. According to this position, a long list of enemies of God—among them secularists, abortionists, humanists, and similar groups—are ultimately responsible for the attacks.

On the other side are those who suggest that no one is to blame for what happened in those great tragedies. Stuff just happens. The disasters of life are random events, having no logic, reason, or purpose. Disaster is merely part of life, so don't try to figure it out. Just deal with it and go on.

Still others suggest that God was directly involved; disaster comes from the hand of God. Another position is that all disasters can be traced to humanity; we are somehow at fault.

So who *is* to blame? Jesus takes up this question in Luke 13, and his answer is not what you would expect. Jesus begins his discussion with stories of two disasters. The first involves Pilate and the Galileans, who were known as a rebellious and stubborn people. Galilee was, in fact, the home of many of the Zealots, a group of Jews who were committed to overthrowing the Roman government by force.

Apparently, a plot was hatched among the Galileans

to do something terrible to the Roman authorities. Pilate discovered the plot and waited for the plotters to come to Jerusalem to offer sacrifices at the temple. While they were offering their sacrifices, his soldiers rushed into the very courts reserved for Jewish men and killed them. When the Galileans least expected it and in a place where they thought they were safe, they were struck down. As a result, their blood was mixed with the blood of their sacrifices. Such a death was considered a sacrilege, especially at the hands of Gentiles in the place where Gentiles were not to be found.

In the second story Jesus mentions a disastrous accident that must have been widely known, involving a rather famous tower of Jerusalem that had given way and toppled over, crushing some who happened to be passing by at that moment. Unlike the first story, in which people were slaughtered by an act of human aggression, the second story concerns people who were killed simply because they were in or near the tower at the wrong time. Both stories—one about great personal suffering, the other about inexplicable personal disaster—raise the same question. Who is to blame?

After telling the story of the Galileans, Jesus, anticipating the thoughts of his listeners, asks, "Do you think that these Galileans were worse sinners than all the other Galileans because they suffered this way?" Knowing that prosperity was to reward righteousness, and evil in life was to follow sin, the listeners could well have thought, "Yes, they were worse sinners. Look at the way in which they died."

Sinners and debtors

The Greek word used in Luke that the English Bible usually translates as "sinners" can refer to two different meanings. First, it can refer to a non-observant Jew, that is, someone who is Jewish but did not practice all the details of the law. Perhaps this offender against ritual did not keep a kosher table, or neglected pilgrimage to the Jerusalem temple for all the required feasts, or did not follow all the Sabbath observance rules. In the eyes of orthodox Jews such men and women indeed would be called "sinners." Jesus may have been asking, "Do you think these Galileans died at the altar in the temple because they did not do all that they were supposed to do, so God judged them in a terrible way?" If it were shown that the dead Galileans were such sinners, good Jews would have responded with a hearty, "Amen and amen. They deserved it!"

The second meaning of the word *sinners* refers to lawbreakers of the worst sort. It is used to describe some of the people with whom Jesus associated—"tax collectors and sinners." His critics here would have meant to use it to describe the worst kind of sinners possible—people with whom no decent rabbi should have even the most remote connection. So Jesus may have been asking, "Do you think that because these Galileans were the worst kind of sinners possible that God finally judged them?" Again, the Jews' answer would have been, "If they were, they got what they deserved!"

At the end of the story about the falling tower, Jesus asks the same question but with a twist: "Do you think they were more guilty than all the others living in Jerusalem?" Instead of using the word *sinners* he uses the word *guilty*, the basic meaning of which is to be in deep indebtedness to someone.

Sinners are indebted to God. Many people believe that over time you accumulate the "sin debt" with God, and when the debt gets large enough God zaps you with his judgment. This thinking was common among the Jews of Jesus' day. It was the thinking centuries before that was expressed by the friends of Job.

Job had lost almost everything, and a few of his closest friends tried to encourage him. Their main message, however, was that Job had better search his life to see what terrible sin he had committed to justify the horrible things that had happened to him. Eliphaz captures the essence of this argument in his conversation with Job. The comments in italics are mine.

> Is it for your piety that he rebukes you and brings charges against you? *(The implied answer is "Of course not!")*

Is not your wickedness great? *(This is why you
have been judged. You have accumulated a large
debt before God.)*

Are not your sins endless? *(This is the reason
why you are in such trouble. Then Eliphaz lists the
sins of Job. With each additional sin the debt gets
larger until God has had enough and decides to
punish Job.)*

You demanded security from your brothers
for no reason;

you stripped men of their clothing, leaving
them naked.

You gave no water to the weary and you with-
held food from the hungry, though you were a
powerful man owning land—an honored man,
living on it.

And you sent widows away empty-handed
and broke the strength of the fatherless.

That is why snares are all around you, why
sudden peril terrifies you,

why it is so dark you cannot see, and why a
flood of water covers you.

—Job 22:4–11

According to Eliphaz, Job had accumulated a large
debt to God over time, and God finally decided to
punish him. Who was to blame for Job's suffering? Job
was to blame, and he was getting what he deserved. In

Jewish thinking of that day, when terrible personal suffering came, it was rooted in the sufferer's guilt before God; when inexplicable natural disaster happened, it could be traced to the corporate sin of the people who were affected by the tragedy.

Why were the Galileans of Jesus' day killed? Because they were worse sinners than anyone else, and God had had enough. Why were the eighteen people killed in the tower? Because they had accumulated a great debt of sin, and the falling tower was God's judgment against them.

Jesus, though, had a different perspective, and his answer must have been shocking to his listeners: "I tell you, no." Indicating emphasis, in the Greek text, the word *no* comes first—"*No*, I tell you." Jesus' statement contradicted the thinking of everyone present. It must have seemed like heresy! His answer went against the grain of accepted theology at that time. We are not told what the listeners were thinking, but their minds must have been spinning. They probably couldn't believe what they'd just heard. "You mean to tell me that those Galileans who died were not worse sinners than us? You mean to tell me that the eighteen people who were killed in the tower of Siloam were not more guilty than we are? Rubbish! Heresy!" But this is precisely what Jesus was saying.

Those of us reading the story in the twenty-first century heave a sigh of relief. When towers fall and suffering comes into our lives, it doesn't mean that we're worse sinners than those who escape such tragedies. This is good news about disasters and about the way God works. But as is often the case with Jesus, the good news is followed by bad news. Jesus shifts the focus of the conversation: "But unless you repent, you too will perish." The real question, then, is not, "Who is to blame?" The real question is, "What about you? Are you ready to die?" The real issue is not about others—the real issue is about you. In this brief statement, Jesus reminds us of several important truths.

We are all sinners

It's easy to look at others and see their sins. It's more difficult to see our own sins. In truth, we are all sinners. Paul, in the book of Romans, suggests that there are two kinds of sinners: religious sinners and non-religious sinners. But we are all sinners (comments again appear in italics):

> What shall we conclude then? Are we any better? (*Are Jews who observe the law any better than those who do not observe the law. This is similar to the stories that Jesus told about the falling tower and the Galileans*). Not at all! We have already made the charge that Jews and Gentiles alike are all under sin. As it is written:

"There is no one righteous, not even one;
There is no one who understands,
no one who seeks God."

—Romans 3:9–11

This is a most unflattering passage, which describes the true condition of every human on the earth. We prefer to sit in judgment of others, compiling a list of the worst sinners. But we fail to see that we are just as bad. We all, in fact, deserve to have towers fall on us. We are all indebted to God; we are all guilty before God.

We all need to repent

Jesus states that unless we repent we will also perish. What is repentance? It's a change of heart and mind that leads to a change of direction—a 180-degree change. Repentance is more than being sorry for your sin; it is turning away from your sin, and it leads to a dramatic change of life.

Paul states, "Godly sorrow brings repentance that leads to salvation and leaves no regret, but worldly sorrow brings death" (2 Corinthians 7:10). Disaster provides a most appropriate time to examine our own lives and to repent of all the sin that has accumulated.

We need to repent while there is time

After answering the question of blame and calling on us to repent, Jesus tells a parable:

> A man had a fig tree, planted in his vineyard, and he went to look for fruit on it, but did not find any. So he said to the man who took care of the vineyard, "For three years now I've been coming to look for fruit on this fig tree and haven't found any. Cut it down! Why should it use up the soil?"
>
> "Sir," the man replied, "leave it alone for one more year, and I'll dig around it and fertilize it. If it bears fruit next year, fine! If not, then cut it down."
>
> —Luke 13:6–9

In this parable, we are the fig tree; the person who comes looking for fruit is death; God is the gardener. When death comes looking for us, God responds by saying, "Wait a minute. Let me dig around the tree. Let me work the soil. Let me fertilize the ground." God is the God of the second chance. If we got what we deserved we'd all end up in hell. But God is patient and longsuffering, working with us so that we will bear fruit.

But God is also the God of the last chance. He says, "If it bears fruit next year, fine! If not, then cut it down."

We are all living somewhere between the second chance and the last chance.

"What about you?" Jesus said. "Are you ready to die?"

Shortly after I was diagnosed with likely ALS, I began to take seriously this particular teaching of Jesus. I started to examine my own life. Had I allowed sins to pile up? Did I need to practice repentance in any area of my life? I knew that my disease was not the direct result of personal sin, but did I need to flush the clutter out of my life?

As I prayed about this, several people came to mind, people I may have offended. I decided that if I was going to die, I wanted to die with a clean conscience before God and others.

The first person who came to mind was Bob Jones III, president of Bob Jones University. I was graduated from this institution with a B.A. and an M.A. While I received a good education there, I've been at odds with some of their stands on issues. I felt, for instance, that they had been very slow to come to terms with biblical principles of racial equality. I felt, too, that their teaching on separation from the world wasn't biblical at all. Consequently, I've been critical and cynical in comments about the University. I have, in fact, a considerable stack of letters from them, including one that states that I am no longer welcome to visit the campus.

I've worn this ban as a badge of honor.

But was this a right attitude?

As I reflected on my disease and my relationship with Bob Jones University, I realized I was good at judging them but not very good at judging my own "superior" attitude. So I called Bob and asked his forgiveness for things I had said and done to offend him and the University.

As I prayed about repentance, another person who came to mind was Jerry Falwell. I worked for Jerry for over fourteen years, and he had a profound influence on my life. I consider him a friend and dear brother, but I don't agree with everything he says and does. Over the years I've been publicly critical of Jerry. At times I've distanced myself from him, feeling that his emphasis on political involvement by pastors was not only hurting the church but lacked a clear biblical mandate.

Several years ago, Cal Thomas and I wrote a book called *Blinded by Might: Can the Religious Right Save America?* (Grand Rapids: Zondervan, 1999). In this volume we reflected on our days with the Moral Majority, looking at some ways in which we thought the movement had not lived up to its ideals. Jerry was not at all pleased with the book and its tone. He was, in fact, deeply offended, although he had never directly said so to me or to anyone else. Prompted by the Holy Spirit, I called Jerry and asked his forgiveness for all the things I had said and done over the years that had offended and hurt him. Later I had the opportunity to preach at Thomas Road Baptist Church, where Jerry pastors, and

I asked forgiveness of the congregation as well. It was not a matter of backing down from principle or not telling the truth in love to a brother in Christ. We as Christians are to live under more stringent standards than the world in the way we think and speak.

The third person who came to mind was James Dobson. He was highly offended by the book I wrote with Cal. I'd spent a day with him and several of his key people discussing it. Although we did not come to a mutual agreement, it had been a healthy meeting. We met again, and in the process began developing a friendship. Jim was one of the first people to call me after the news spread of my diagnosis. He wanted me to know that he and Shirley were praying for my healing. I then asked him to forgive me for anything I had said and done that offended and hurt him. He, too, asked forgiveness for things he'd said that had hurt me.

I struggled with repentance, thinking that some of the people would take my apology as an admission that I was wrong on some issues and that they were right. But in the end, whether I'm seen as right or wrong in the eyes of others doesn't matter. I answer to God only for myself. What matters is that I have been too quick to see the "faults" of others and too slow to see my own. I had lost sight of my own need for repentance and my responsibility before God for my brothers and sisters in Christ. I had forgotten that these brothers with whom I had disagreements were, in fact, brothers.

I had forgotten that we are all living between the second and last chances. We are not all to blame when buildings tumble, but that fact should humble us. It should remind us of the brevity and uncertainty of life. It should cause us to examine our own lives. It should cause us to ask, "What if I knew that one week from now my tower would fall? What would I do between now and then?"

Whatever I would do—I should do it!

chapter seven

Is It Right to Punish the Terrorists and Go to War?

Hear me, O God, as I voice my complaint;
   protect my life from the threat of the enemy.
Hide me from the conspiracy of the wicked,
   from that noisy crowd of evildoers.

They sharpen their tongues like swords
   and aim their words like deadly arrows.
They shoot from ambush at the innocent
   man;
      they shoot at him suddenly, without fear.
They encourage each other in evil plans,
   they talk about hiding their snares;
   they say, "Who will see them?"
They plot injustice and say,
   "We have devised a perfect plan!"

Surely the mind and heart of man are
    cunning.

But God will shoot them with arrows;
    suddenly they will be struck down.
He will turn their own tongues against them
    and bring them to ruin;
    all who see them will shake their heads in
    scorn.

All mankind will fear;
    they will proclaim the works of God
    and ponder what he has done.
Let the righteous rejoice in the LORD
    and take refuge in him;
    let all the upright in heart praise him!
                              —Psalm 64

STANDING AT THE EDGE of Ground Zero, Psalm 64 easily
comes to mind.

While I was there, I spoke with a New York City police captain. A big Irishman, he'd been on duty continually since the Trade Towers had fallen, and he was
still having a hard time taking it all in. Several of his
friends were buried under the rubble. He still held out
some hope that one of them might yet be found alive.
His face wore a blank expression as he looked at the
mountain of debris. We talked about his friends and

the other police officers, and how they all were doing in light of what had happened.

"I tell you," he said, "I hope we get the people who did this. I hope we wipe out Afghanistan. 'Nuke' them, as far as I am concerned."

If we had been standing outside the building where my church meets in Grand Rapids, Michigan, the officer's words would have sounded harsh and insensitive. But in that time and space, at the gravesite of thousands of people who were buried under twenty-three acres of destruction, the emotion behind the words seemed perfectly normal and appropriate.

It can be difficult for us as Christians to temper our righteous passions and listen to Scripture.

Consider, for example, the following passage:

> Everyone must submit himself to the governing authorities, for there is no authority except that which God has established. The authorities that exist have been established by God.
>
> Consequently, he who rebels against authority is rebelling against what God has instituted, and those who do so will bring judgment on themselves.
>
> For rulers hold no terror for those who do right, but for those who do wrong. Do you want to be free from fear of the one in authority? Then do what is right and he will commend you.

For he is God's servant to do you good. But if you do wrong, be afraid, for he does not bear the sword for nothing. He is God's servant, an agent of wrath to bring punishment on the wrongdoer.

Therefore, it is necessary to submit to the authorities, not only because of possible punishment but also because of conscience.

—Romans 13:1–5

Is the punishment of terrorists, then, biblical? Is the war we are fighting against terrorists a righteous one? Several truths in Romans 13 shape our understanding of authority, government, crime, and punishment.

First, all human government derives its authority from God: "There is no authority except that which God has established" (v. 1). Government officials are called the "servants" of God (v. 4).

Second, human government exists to promote an ordered and structured society, so it must punish evil. As an individual citizen, I do not have the right to punish people who violate civil laws. Punishing those who break the law is the exclusive right of the government. It is, in fact, one of the reasons that government exists.

Third, God gives the "sword" to the government as a means of punishing evil. The sword represents the ultimate punishment—the taking of a human life. When the government exercises its right to punish evil, it is acting as "an agent of wrath to bring punishment on the wrongdoer"(v. 4).

Does the United States have the right, then, to go after terrorists and bring them to justice? Absolutely. And it is the responsibility of other governments to assist in this endeavor. Bringing wrongdoers to justice and punishing them is the God-given purpose of government. When governments do so, even by using the sword, they act within the boundaries of Scripture.

Just war and true justice

Scripture does not, however, issue a blanket endorsement of every use of the sword and every possible means that might be used to accomplish the task. Principled biblical guidelines must be observed, even when waging war.

War is a harsh reality in this broken and sinful world: There is "a time to love and a time to hate, a time for war and a time for peace" (Ecclesiastes 3:8). Jesus, too, predicted that as we approached the end of the world, wars would become more frequent (Matthew 24:1–8).

At issue, then, is, "When is the time for war?"

The Roman Catholic Church (and the Calvinist tradition of Protestantism) advocates the theory of "just war," a teaching with roots in Scripture. The premise is that while war is a terrible endeavor, circumstances nonetheless occur under which war is justified and necessary. Bishop Augustine of Hippo (354–430) believed, for example, that war was both the result of sin and the remedy for sin. In other words, under certain circumstances war could be used to restrain sin.

Over the centuries, the church developed the theory of just war based on certain principles first enunciated by Augustine. The following statement of those principles is taken from "A Pastoral Letter on War and Peace," which was published by the United States National Conference of Catholic Bishops on May 3, 1983. (See *Catholics and Nuclear War*, ed. Philip J. Murnion, New York: Crossroad, 1983, 276–80. Reformed Protestant statements of the just war theory vary little from this Catholic statement.):

> *Just cause.* War is permissible only to confront "a real and certain danger," i.e., to protect innocent life, to preserve conditions necessary for decent human existence, and to secure basic human rights.

> *Competent authority.* In the Catholic tradition, the right to use force has always been joined to the common good; war must be declared by those with the responsibility for public order, not by private groups or individuals.

> *Comparative justice.* This principle deals with the

issue of whether or not war is the only means of serving justice: which side is sufficiently right in a dispute, and are the values at stake critical enough to override the presumption against war?

Right intention. Legitimate intent for waging war consists only of those reasons as set forth above as being a just cause. During the conflict, right intention means pursuit of peace and reconciliation, including the avoidance of destructive acts or imposition of unreasonable conditions (e.g., unconditional surrender).

Last resort. Resorting to war is justified only after all peaceful alternatives have been exhausted.

Probability of success. A difficult criterion to assess, its purpose is to prevent irrational resort to force or hopeless resistance when the outcome will be either clearly disproportionate or futile.

Proportionality. The damage to be inflicted and the costs incurred by war must be proportionate to the good that is expected to result by taking up arms.

While recognizing that we live in a sinful world and while understanding the New York City policeman's desire to get even with the terrorists, we must nonetheless exercise caution about national and international decisions to wage war. The above principles should be carefully considered, for it is our responsibility to promote justice, not revenge.

In promoting justice, we must keep in mind another biblical mandate—one that is especially difficult to apply in light of September 11, 2001:

> But I tell you who hear me: Love your enemies, do good to those who hate you, bless those who curse you, pray for those who mistreat you. . . . But love your enemies, do good to them, and lend to them without expecting to get anything back. Then your reward will be great, and you will be sons of the Most High, because he is kind to the ungrateful and wicked. Be merciful, just as your Father is merciful.
>
> —Luke 6:27, 35–36

What does this mean? Are we to love Osama bin Laden? Are we to do good to those who hate us and America? If so, it seems to contradict the notions about a just war and the need for justice. And what is to be gained by loving and doing good to people who desire to destroy us? If we do good to them, they will more easily harm us.

One could make a moral argument that killing the terrorist leaders is, in fact, a good act since it will prevent future loss of innocent life. But in Luke 6, Jesus is not talking about the greater good. He's talking about the good *of our enemies.*

This teaching of Jesus must be understood in context and in light of the rest of the teaching of Scripture. Jesus lived in a Jewish culture with a very narrow worldview, one that placed people into two categories. The Jews inhabited one category, and the rest of the world, the *goyim,* or Gentiles, inhabited the other. The Jews believed themselves to be obligated under Torah to love those who were of Israel—namely Jews. That was the extent of their obligation to love. The rest of the world, whom they described as "dogs," could be hated.

Loving and loving justice

Jesus completely contradicted this worldview and called upon the Jews to love everybody. Jesus affirmed Torah, which says to love your neighbor. Then, however, he expanded the definition of *neighbor* to include all of humanity. So instead of hating the Gentiles, Jesus called upon the Jews to love them, do good to them, and lend to them without expecting anything in return. In other words, Jesus taught that the Jews were to treat the Gentiles as they treated their Jewish neighbors.

This was revolutionary teaching.

How, then, does this teaching apply to the current situation? The first, central principle that stands at the forefront in Jesus' teaching is that Osama bin Laden and his terrorist allies are human beings created in the image of God. They may be our enemies, committed to destroying us, but they are human beings upon whom God sends both rain and sun. Jesus said that God "is kind to the ungrateful and wicked" (v. 35).

Second, as a nation we can bring our enemies to justice as evildoers who must be restrained. Waging war against them is not a violation of the teaching of Jesus. It is rather the proportionate response of governments defending their citizens against further death and destruction.

Third, given the complexities and particular difficulties of the situation, we must love and do good to the extent that we have the wisdom to know what is "good." We can increase discernment by praying for those who hate us, by dealing with the underlying causes of terror—poverty and injustice—and by performing good acts whenever possible. The food drops that accompanied the bombing of Afghanistan are an example of doing good while at the same time waging war. Mistakes were made in executing those drops because of the limits of the planners' wisdom and knowledge of the realities of Afghan society at the time. The drops were not Christian programs, and some motives might have been as political as they were humanitarian. But the action fit well within just war principles and the specific teachings of Christ.

In spite of biblical principles and guidelines for engaging an enemy, believers may experience widely ambivalent feelings in regard to war. As believers, we have two areas of responsibility—to God and to the government. In times of war, these responsibilities frequently must be held in tension.

This tension can be especially difficult to sort out in relation to the Middle East, where the Jewish state and the Palestinian Authority are in perennial serious conflict. I've been to Bethlehem multiple times and have become acquainted with believers in that city. Palestinians suffer under the policies of the Israeli government and are bombed on a regular basis. Many people there have been made homeless by missiles made in the United States and delivered by the Israelis. Palestinian Muslims there have some reason to feel hatred or bitterness toward America, and some Christian Palestinians share their feelings.

On the other hand, a great many other believers in Israel support the actions of the Israeli government. The sympathies of our brothers and sisters in Christ who reside in Israel fall on both sides of this conflict. Thus it is not surprising that believers elsewhere, including the United States, have mixed feelings if they know much about recent history.

The same is true in regard to the current war against terrorism in Afghanistan. Afghanistan, Pakistan, and India also are homes for many believers. It is doubtful that many Afghan Christians supported the Taliban, which intensely persecuted them. But regional politics are seldom cut-and-dried, and Christians have various stakes in their communities. We certainly cannot be so blind as to suppose that we can understand the sympathies of believers in other countries. Believers reside in all countries, and all believers are our brothers and sisters. We should be praying for them and doing all that we can to help them, even if we are at war with the countries in which they live and regardless of where our political understandings may vary.

Loving our enemies while simultaneously seeking justice and inflicting punishment upon their criminal governments is, indeed, a difficult task. But, as in all things, we can look to God as our model. God, at times, chastises his children. He allows us to suffer consequences of our own behavior. Yet God never stops loving us. As children of God, we must endeavor to do no less.

chapter eight

OF WHOM SHALL I
BE AFRAID?

The LORD is my light and my salvation—
    whom shall I fear?
The LORD is the stronghold of my life—
    of whom shall I be afraid?
When evil men advance against me
    to devour my flesh,
when my enemies and my foes attack me,
    they will stumble and fall.
Though an army besiege me,
    my heart will not fear;
though war break out against me,
    even then will I be confident.

—Psalm 27:1–3

FEAR IS PARALYZING. I talked recently with a woman who
had just buried her husband of over forty years. I asked
how she was doing. "I'm afraid," she immediately

responded. She was afraid of the future and how she would survive without her husband.

As I walked around Ground Zero and talked with people, it became obvious that many of them were afraid. Fear had infiltrated the entire city of New York. Frequently I'd ask the people I met, "How is the city doing?" The nearly unanimous answer was, "People are afraid." They were afraid to go in high-rise buildings, afraid to get on airplanes, afraid of when the next attack might come. Even those who ventured out to ball games, the theatre, restaurants, and shops did so with a certain measure of fear.

The Bible addresses fear. Most often it tells us, "Fear not." The words *fear not* appear 365 times in Scripture. The frequency suggests two things.

First, fear is a major problem for humans; second, God doesn't want us to live in fear. Consequently, he repeatedly reminds us that living in fear is not his plan for us. *Fear not* is more than a suggestion—it's a command, something we are to obey. When God gives a command, he gives us the strength to obey that command. However difficult it may seem to overcome fear, it's not impossible.

At the end of Psalm 27, the writer gives us the key to overcoming our fears: "I am still confident of this" (v. 13). The opposite of fear is confidence, and confidence is another word for faith. In order to overcome our fears, then, we must develop our faith and confidence. Psalm 27 in its entirety is about developing that faith and confidence.

Developing faith begins with a choice: Will I choose to focus on circumstances that fuel my fears or will I choose to focus on God who promises to alleviate my fears? If we focus on the darkness, the rubble, the distress, or the brokenness, then the consequence will be a life filled with fear. But if we focus on God and not the current situation, then the consequence will be deliverance from fear.

Faith, then, begins with choice of focus—my circumstances or the Lord? Psalm 27 commences by reminding us of that choice and giving us reasons to trust God in spite of the circumstances.

"The Lord is my light"

The Bible often speaks of God as light. But this is the only time in the entire Bible where God is called *my light*. When darkness surrounds me I can still see, because the Lord is *my* light. Have you ever tried to walk through a darkened room? You cautiously grope with one foot at a time, feeling to determine whether you can safely set down your foot for another step. If you're not careful, you'll stub your toe or trip and hurt yourself. Progress is slow and dangerous in the dark. When we are forced to walk in darkness, the greatest obstacle is usually our own fear. But the psalmist proclaims, "The

LORD is my light." God illuminates our path and eliminates our fears.

"The Lord is my salvation"

The word *salvation* is not used here in the sense of "spiritual" salvation. Rather, it is physical salvation, referring to deliverance from danger. When we are drowning and there is no one to save us, we can count on God to deliver us from the danger. In the darkness he allows me to see the way; when I am drowning, he throws me a lifeline and saves me.

"The Lord is the stronghold of my life"

The word *stronghold* describes a mountain fortress. In ancient times, the best place to build a fortification was on a mountain. Attacking enemies would be forced to fight from the low ground up the mountain. In battle, whoever has the higher ground has a superior position. As the attempt to root out Taliban fighters from the caves of Afghanistan showed, a mountain stronghold also is a secure place to hide, a place into which the enemy cannot easily see. The psalmist declares that God is the stronghold of our lives. He is our hiding place, our security, our defensive perimeter.

The Lord is our light, our salvation, our stronghold. Is it any wonder then that the psalmist's next thought is

"Whom shall I fear? . . . Of whom shall I be afraid?" There is no need for fear because God is on our side. He guides us through the night, he rescues us from drowning, he gives refuge to us in his mountain fortress. No one and nothing can overcome us when we trust in God. The psalmist is so certain of God's protection that he makes some incredibly confident statements.

> When evil men advance against me
>   to devour my flesh,
> when my enemies and my foes attack me,
>   they will stumble and fall.
> Though an army besiege me,
>   my heart will not fear;
> though war break out against me,
>   even then will I be confident.
>   —Psalm 27:2–3

In these verses, the psalmist is speaking of the future. These events have not happened. But if they do, the writer is confident. He knows that God will deliver him and that his enemies will "stumble and fall." He is declaring his confidence in God ahead of time, verbalizing his faith, because faith needs to be spoken. "If you confess with your mouth, 'Jesus is Lord,' and believe in your heart that God raised him from the dead, you will be saved" (Romans 10:9). Faith is both believing and confessing.

Words, then, are important to our faith journey. Too often we use words of defeat and discouragement, doubting that God will guide, save, and protect us. The psalmist teaches us that, instead of using a language of doubt, we must confidently declare that it is our infinite and eternal God who is speaking. We must verbally testify to ourselves and whoever else might be interested what he will do on our behalf.

Finding God's presence

In the first days after I was diagnosed with motor neuron disease, I had all sorts of fears—fear of the future, fear of losing my voice and not being able to preach, fear of being unable to swallow, fear of being unable to breathe. Then I came across some verses that I memorized, taping them to the bathroom mirror so I'd see them when I first awoke every morning:

> God has said, "Never will I leave you; never will I forsake you." So we say with confidence, "The Lord is my helper; I will not be afraid. What can man do to me?"
> —Hebrews 13:5b–6

Whenever I am overcome with fear, I call a ten-minute time-out and repeat these verses over and over for the entire ten minutes. As I speak these words in the face of my fears, God uses them to alleviate my panic and give me hope. I must admit, however, that often the words of Scripture seem empty when compared to the gripping dread that at times invades my mind. Even when it doesn't seem to help, I repeat the words out loud. The Holy Spirit seems to powerfully apply the promises of God when I declare them aloud before my own heart. Repeated over and over, they begin to sink into my mind and soul.

The second step in developing your faith is to cultivate personal intimacy with the Lord. David expresses the hunger for this closeness when he writes of his search for the Lord in Psalm 27:

> One thing I ask of the LORD,
>   this is what I seek:
> that I may dwell in the house of the LORD
>   all the days of my life,
> to gaze upon the beauty of the LORD
>   and to seek him in his temple.
> —Psalm 27:4

David states that the one consuming passion of his life is to live every day as close to God as he possibly can. How close? He wants to live in the tent of the tabernacle every day. The tent was the dwelling place of God on the earth, and David wants to spend the rest of his life there.

In the tent, he wants "to gaze upon the beauty of the LORD." The word *gaze* means to linger, stay behind, or cling to something. And as he lingers, David wants to see the beauty of the Lord, the word *beauty* meaning the pleasantness, the goodness, or the gracefulness of God. David adds that he wants to seek God, the word *seek* meaning to reflect on something, to meditate, or think about something.

Thus, faith is not only a choice to focus on God; it is an ongoing passion that drives us to pursue intimate relationship with God. Faith says, "I want to live in your presence, to linger before your goodness, to see your grace, and to meditate upon you for the rest of my life."

By reading a few additional lines of the above psalm, three ideas about faith can be discovered:

> For in the day of trouble
>   he will keep me safe in his dwelling;
> he will hide me in the shelter of his
>   tabernacle
> and set me high upon a rock.
>   —Psalm 27:5

Faith lives close to God

People who are consumed with fear and uncertainty about the future almost always live a long distance from

God. The closer you get to God, the more confident you become about who God is and what he has promised. The closer you get to God, the more your fears subside. Psalm 27:5 says that it is in his dwelling and tabernacle that God sets us upon a rock.

Faith meditates on the character of God

When we get into trouble, we often write our own strategy for getting out of trouble. We list our strengths, the people who might be able to help us, our goals and objectives. While strategy certainly has its place, we should first begin by listing all the attributes of God and then spending time thinking about them. In the day of trouble, the psalmist is in a position of total dependence on God.

Faith declares the deliverance of God

God promises to do three things for us when we're in trouble: First, he will keep us safe; second, he will hide us in his shelter; and third, he will set us upon a rock. When we are developing our faith, we must continually repeat the promises of God. God will protect us—no matter what.

David says in Psalm 27:6, "Then my head will be exalted above the enemies who surround me; at his tabernacle will I sacrifice with shouts of joy; I will sing and make music to the LORD." Whatever you're facing, the day will come when you'll sing again with shouts of joy. God has promised.

The first part of Psalm 27 is filled with hope and faith: "Of whom shall I be afraid?" Even before the Lord delivers him, David speaks of that deliverance as if it had already happened. He has the kind of faith that all believers—even me—want when we are in trouble.

While faith is developed through focusing on God and through a personal relationship with God, faith is strengthened through prayer. David's prayer, which begins in Psalm 27:7, seems to be such a contrast from the ebullient confidence of the first part of the psalm. When he gets to the prayer, we see that in the unspecified outward realities, David does not feel so confident after all.

> Hear my voice when I call, O LORD;
>   be merciful to me and answer me.
> My heart says of you, "Seek his face!"
>   Your face, LORD, I will seek.
> Do not hide your face from me,
>   do not turn your servant away in anger;
>   you have been my helper.
> Do not reject me or forsake me,
>   O God my Savior.
> Though my father and mother forsake me,
>   the LORD will receive me.

Do not turn me over to the desire of my foes,
   for false witnesses rise up against me,
   breathing out violence.
                              —Psalm 27:7–10, 12

This is an honest, gut-level prayer. While David is confident of God's protection in his life, his faith remains weak. David pours out his heart to God: "Hear me. Don't reject me. Be merciful to me. Don't turn your face from me. Don't let my enemies overcome me. Teach me your way." Faith is not the absence of doubt; it is admitting your doubt to God and asking him for help.

Is your faith weak? Do you doubt God? Then pray—and be honest when you pray. Tell God all about your fears and doubts.

In spite of David's fears, he concludes the psalm with the promise that he will see the "goodness" of God while he is alive:

I am still confident of this:
   I will see the goodness of the LORD
   in the land of the living.
Wait for the LORD;
   be strong and take heart
   and wait for the LORD.
                              —Psalm 27:13–14

David concludes with this compelling truth—God is on our side. He will take care of us. Therefore, let us wait for him. If you are struggling with God and your circumstances, make a sign and put it where you can see it every day:

**God is on our side,
and the God
who is on our side
is good.**

chapter nine

HOW DO YOU FACE AND CONQUER YOUR FEARS?

God is our refuge and strength,
  an ever-present help in trouble.
Therefore we will not fear, though the earth
  give way
and the mountains fall into the heart of the
  sea,
though its waters roar and foam
  and the mountains quake with their surging.
                                      —Psalm 46:1–3

CHAPTER 8 EXPLORED the truth that we should not fear because God is on our side. This is easy to accept in theory, but hard to live in practice. The realities of our present circumstances often mitigate against really trusting God. So how do we deal with our fears? How can we overcome them?

Fear is a natural component of life, and for a great many people in America and Europe, fears have increased since

the attacks of September 11. Given some of the news
events, it seems not much of an exaggeration to say
that some Americans became obsessed with fear—fear
of flying; fear of anthrax-contaminated mail; fear of
high-rise buildings; fear of going to crowded shopping
malls; fear of the future in general, of war, of disease,
of recession and unemployment, of sending kids off
to college.

In the face of all these fears, the Bible gives us the
answer to overcoming them—not just a few of them
but all of them.

The writer of Psalm 46 proclaims that "therefore we
will not fear" (v. 2). Then he adds the circumstances
under which he makes this statement—he talks about
the mountains falling into the sea and the earth crum-
bling. Such a calamity is likely an allusion to the creation story, wherein God brings order out of chaos:
"Now the earth was formless and empty, darkness was
over the surface of the deep"(Genesis 1:2a). On the
third day of creation, God separated the waters and
formed the dry ground. "And God said, 'Let the water
under the sky be gathered to one place, and let dry
ground appear'" (v. 9). The mountains and the ground
were actually taken out of the sea as God gathered the
seas and restricted their boundaries.

What if that process were reversed? wonders the
writer of Psalm 46. That would be just about the ultimate in natural calamities. Even if the mountains were

to go back into the sea from whence they were removed at creation, the psalmist would not be afraid. In the greatest chaos, those who are hidden in God's mountain stronghold need not fear.

Fearlessness in the face of utter chaos goes against our inclination, but a key to dealing with fear is to focus beyond the monster that looms so deadly, and focus instead on God. In this psalm there are three realities about God that enable us to rise above our fears.

First, God is our protection. "God is our refuge" (Psalm 46:1a). The word *refuge* refers to a shelter in time of danger. When the mountains are collapsing into the sea and the earth is giving way, God is a shelter who is able to protect us. Later in the psalm the writer states, "The LORD Almighty is with us; the God of Jacob is our fortress" (vv. 7, 11).

Second, God is always with us. He is "an ever-present help in trouble" (46:1b). God is ever present. He doesn't go out for lunch, nor does he take a vacation, nor does he doze over a cup of coffee. No matter what happens in our lives, we can be sure that God is present. An alternate translation for Psalm 46:1 could be, "As a help in distress, he is thoroughly proved." Or another wording might be, "He is abundantly available for help in tight spaces." The world may crumble around us and the towers of our lives may fall, but God is with us and he is abundantly available.

Third, God is powerful. "The LORD Almighty is with us" (vv. 7, 11). This statement is repeated, emphasizing that the God who is with us and protects us is "almighty." God's infinite might is foundational to the other truths about who he is. If he is not almighty, then it is less likely that he can protect us when our world falls apart. If he is not almighty and omnipresent, then it is unlikely that His presence will be able to drive away our fears. But if he really is almighty—and he is—then nothing can harm us.

Christians who have read the Bible and have lived before the face of God know these truths. The challenge is to put the concepts and past experiences of God's goodness into practice when our world goes into chaos. The people who are most confident about these truths usually are those who are not facing great difficulties in their lives. Those of us who face immense problems struggle greatly to believe and put these truths into practice in order to conquer our fears.

The art of being still

So how do we practice these truths?

David gives good advice: "Be still, and know that I am God; I will be exalted among the nations, I will be exalted in the earth" (46:10). The verb translated *be still* means to cease from striving or to stop running. It means, in the vernacular of our time, "chill out." When the world falls apart, chill out and turn to God.

After the events of September 11, 2001, anyone with a television set in a non-Islamic nation was bombarded by images of planes smashing into towers and footage of the towers collapsing. Each day most of us rushed home to turn on the news and learn the latest developments—anthrax, the war in Afghanistan, the latest threats to our security. We were held hostage by the media, almost addicted to getting the latest news. But as long as we're addicted to the next event, we do not have time for God. As long as we fill our minds with the latest news—news that frequently is oriented to our fears—we'll never be able to chill out.

Several years ago, I decided to take a break from the media. For three months, I unplugged the e-mail, the television, and the radio. I didn't read newspapers or magazines. The only book I read was the Bible, and I read it completely through during those three months. That was a remarkable period in my life. I was able to listen to God more clearly because I had far fewer distractions.

One need not take so radical an action to turn personal focus on God, but I would suggest that some of our fears derive from the amount of time we spend listening to the wrong voices—while we do not spend adequate time listening to God's voice.

So chill out.

"I will say of the LORD . . ."

A simple way to focus on God's truths instead of our fears is to make them a topic of conversation. When disaster strikes, the human tendency is to let the disaster dominate our conversation. The psalmist offers an alternative topic of discussion:

> He who dwells in the shelter of the Most High
> will rest in the shadow of the Almighty.
> I will say of the LORD, "He is my refuge and
> my fortress,
> my God, in whom I trust."
> —Psalm 91:1–2

Note the emphasis, "I will say of the LORD." The writer makes a choice in regard to his topic, and he chooses to talk about the greatness of God.

About three months after I had been diagnosed with ALS, my wife Lorna and I were at a local coffee shop. The mugs were very heavy, and I commented that I had a hard time lifting them with my right hand. She broke down in tears.

After she regained her composure, I asked her what was wrong.

"Ever since you went to the clinic in Ann Arbor," she said, "that's all you talk about. Every conversation gets to your disease. Couldn't we talk about something else?"

I hadn't even realized that ALS had become my main topic of conversation with my family. The subject had so consumed me, so dominated my thinking, that I couldn't talk about anything else.

What do you talk about? David chose to talk about God rather than his problems.

One practical way to overcome fear is to memorize portions of Scripture that one can bring to mind and repeat over and over when a crisis becomes mind-dominating. Standing at Ground Zero, no words would come to my mind. So I repeated the Word of God: "God is my refuge and strength. He is my fortress." Suddenly the focus of my thinking and my faith was not on human structures, however strong they might have appeared. I knew that the only sure faith is in the God who promises to be my protection when the mountains fall into the sea.

To deal with fear, then, mentally unplug and pay attention to God. Declare the greatness of God in spite of the circumstances and sing about his greatness.

> But I will sing of your strength,
>   in the morning I will sing of your love;
> for you are my fortress,
>   my refuge in times of trouble.
> O my Strength, I sing praise to you;
>   you, O God, are my fortress, my loving God.
>   —Psalm 59:16–17

During the darkest times after I was diagnosed, I looked forward to worshiping with the church. I especially looked forward to the times of singing. At times I was overwhelmed by the message of a song and could not join in. It was enough to allow the Spirit to apply the words. I can't explain the healing of my spirit that occurred in those song services over the weeks. I was lifted by the music and led to thank God for giving me hope for another week.

"How do you face and conquer your fears?" From Scripture, I offer these answers:

- Be still and know God.
- Focus your conversation on God rather than on problems.
- Sing—sing your heart out. Sing about God's strength, his love, his refuge in times of trouble. Yes, sing of God all the day long.

chapter ten

How Do We Praise God at a Time Like This?

I will extol the LORD at all times;
　　his praise will always be on my lips.
My soul will boast in the LORD;
　　let the afflicted hear and rejoice.
Glorify the LORD with me;
　　let us exalt his name together.

I sought the LORD, and he answered me;
　　he delivered me from all my fears.
Those who look to him are radiant;
　　their faces are never covered with shame.
This poor man called, and the LORD heard
　　him;
　　he saved him out of all his troubles.
The face of the LORD is against those who do
　　evil.

The LORD is close to the brokenhearted
and saves those who are crushed in spirit.
—Psalm 34:1–6, 16a, 18

DURING THE FIRST MONTHS after the doctors told me that I likely had amyotrophic lateral sclerosis or ALS, I had great difficulty praying. I just didn't feel like doing it. But as difficult as praying was, praising the Lord was even more difficult. "What's there to praise God about?" I asked myself. Yet Psalm 34 says that we are to extol the Lord *at all times.* His praise is to be *always on our lips.* This is a tall order. Are we really to praise God during disaster? Are we really to praise God during suffering?

The answer is, "Yes."

Some may say, "I know you Christians. You bury your heads in the sand and act as if nothing is wrong. You go around blessing God and thanking him when all around you is the rubble of broken lives and dreams. You're in another world. You just ignore the realities of life and claim you are being spiritual!"

True praise, however, does not ignore the ugly realities of life. True praise is lifted to God from the midst of the chaos and the rubble at our own personal Ground Zero.

The psalmist knows, as does God, that at times it is difficult to praise God. Psalm 34 doesn't ignore realities. The writer lists several circumstances that may rob us of the ability to praise:

- *Fear.* "I sought the Lord, and he answered me; he delivered me from all my fears" (v. 4). Fear is paralyzing. We fear for the future and for the past, fear for our safety and for our children. Fear makes it difficult to praise God.

- *Shame.* "Those who look to him are radiant; their faces are never covered with shame" (v. 5). Living with the shame of past decisions and behavior can rob us of praise. How can we praise God when our lives are filled with guilt and shame?

- *Trouble.* "This poor man called, and the Lord heard him; he saved him out of all his troubles" (v. 6). Trouble distracts us, causing us to focus on the immediate present. It's hard to turn to God in praise when we are in trouble.

- *Evil.* "The face of the Lord is against those who do evil" (v. 16). It's impossible to praise God when sin is in our lives. Thus, sin must be confessed before we can praise God.

- *A crushed spirit.* "The Lord is close to the brokenhearted and saves those who are crushed in spirit" (v. 18). When our hearts have been broken and our spirits crushed, we feel that the very life has been squeezed out of us. At such times it's hard to focus on God.

In spite of all these challenges, we are to praise God: "I will extol the Lord at *all* times." Whether in the face of fear, shame, or trouble, we are to praise God; in the face of trouble, brokenness, and evil, we are to praise God.

Finding reasons to praise

At times, praising God seems impossible, but with God all things are possible. First, consider that God provides help for each difficulty of life. Look at Psalm 34, point by point:

- When we are afraid, God delivers us.
- When we look to God, he removes the shame.
- In trouble, we can call to him and he will deliver us.
- God is against those who do evil, but if we confess our sin, then God is for us.
- When we are brokenhearted and crushed, the Lord is near us.

God's provision for us is reason to praise him. Whatever the obstacle to praise, God will remove it and liberate us to declare his praise.

Second, while our circumstances change, God never changes. He is the same today as he was when the psalmist wrote his poetry, and as he is in all eternity. We change, our situations change, but God never changes. We have yet more reason to praise him.

Third, the God who never changes is with us in the midst of our difficulties and challenges. God does not abandon us when the going gets tough. As you read Psalm 34, underline the words *deliver, save,* and *redeem* each time they occur. The psalmist demonstrates that God is in the business of delivering, saving, and redeeming. The life of Joseph is a testimony to God's ability to deliver, save, and redeem. Although Joseph was sold into slavery by his own brothers, God used this great evil to save and redeem his family from famine. Therefore, God is deserving of our praise, even when we face disaster.

Perhaps you now accept that it is, indeed, possible to praise God in the midst of trouble, even in the midst of disaster. What, though, does it mean to praise God?

In the following three verses, five different Hebrew words describe the praise of God (italics added).

> I will *extol* the Lord at all times; his *praise* will always be on my lips. My soul will *boast* in the Lord; let the afflicted hear and rejoice. *Glorify* the Lord with me; let us *exalt* his name together.
> —Psalm 34:1–3

The first word used for "praise" is *extol*. Literally it means "to bless." The psalm, then, begins, "I will *bless* the Lord at all times." What does it mean to bless God? When God finished creating the world, he blessed it:

"God blessed them and said, 'Be fruitful and increase in number and fill the water in the seas, and let the birds increase on the earth'" (Genesis 1:22). Later God blessed Adam and Eve: "God blessed them and said to them, 'Be fruitful and increase in number; fill the earth and subdue it. Rule over the fish of the sea and the birds of the air and over every living creature that moves on the ground'" (Genesis 1:28).

When God blessed the fish, the birds, and the humans, he was bestowing power upon them to multiply and increase. Thus, the blessing was for success and prosperity. When we bless God, we are declaring him as the source of all power and success.

The traditional Jewish blessing declares, "Blessed are you, God, our God, King of the universe." They then add to the blessing whatever is appropriate for the moment. A blessing given at the meal, for example, would be: "Blessed are you, God, our God, King of the universe, who brings forth bread from the earth." When we bless God we are declaring that God is our source! In the New Testament, James puts it this way: "Every good and every perfect gift is from above, coming down from the Father of the heavenly lights" (James 1:17).

The second Hebrew word used in this psalm to describe praise is the word *praise*: "his *praise* will always be on my lips." *Praise* in this instance means "hallelujah," that is, "His *hallelujah* will always be on my lips." The word *hallelujah* comes from a verb that means "to shine the light on something; to illuminate." Here, it carries the meaning of bringing something into focus so that it can clearly be seen . Note how it's used in the book of Job:

> How I long for the months gone by, for the days when God watched over me, when his lamp *shone upon my head* [this is the word *hallelujah*] and by his light I walked through darkness!
> —Job 29:2–3

When I first came to Grand Rapids I was thirty-seven years old and had a full head of hair. Over the years, because of weather, perhaps, or the stress of pastoral ministry, I've been gradually losing my hair. The rate of hair loss did not seem so noticeable until one day when I was watching the videotape our church broadcasts each week over a local public access television station. The "me" on television looked fine—until I leaned into the television lights. Under the glare of the spotlight my true condition was revealed to the world.

Not many people would fare well under the glare of the spotlight of personal revelation, but when we shine our hallelujahs on God, his perfection is revealed, and we discover his shining character.

There's an interesting secondary meaning for the word *hallelujah*. A verb form of the Hebrew word sometimes can be translated "to behave crazy": "Charge, O

horses! Drive furiously [*hallelujah* as a verb], O chari-
oteers!" (Jeremiah 46:9a). A lot of readers might know
of someone who "drives hallelujah." In stock car rac-
ing, the late Dale Earnhardt might come to mind. Blast-
ing around NASCAR tracks at 190-plus miles an hour,
Earnhardt was known as someone who loved to make
a car do the impossible, not so much to win as for the
sheer joy of competing with his fellow drivers. NASCAR
driver Larry Waltrip once said that "with Dale, every
lap is a controlled crash." He thought nothing of trad-
ing paint and nudging bumpers with other drivers he
knew he could trust "not to do anything stupid." In
his fatal crash it was the vehicle, not Earnhardt, that
came apart.

Off the track Earnhardt also exhibited hallelujah. He
and his business manager, Don Hawk, almost rein-
vented American respect for the sport of stock car rac-
ing through their marketing of "the Intimidator" image.
The two men also changed the hard-drinking, wom-
anizing reputation of the sport with forthright and
outspoken Christian integrity. The crazy exuberance of
hallelujah was a way of life for Earnhardt, and he would
have loved driving furiously in Jeremiah's chariot (a
Monte Carlo chariot, of course) with the top down.
Exhilarating recklessness well illustrates the meaning
of *furious* in the above text from Jeremiah—the chari-
oteers charging with their horses is similar to driving
195 miles per hour around the Charlotte Motor Speed-

way. When we hallelujah God, we are to do it with passion and reckless abandon.

The third word for "praise" is *boast*. Notice that the boast is coming from "my soul," the "real person" of the psalmist. Our mouths can boast about a lot of things, even the Lord. But it only means something if there is a soul that is boasting behind the mouth. If there is, we won't have to worry much about what the mouth says.

When we undergo crisis, we Christians are sometimes so hung up over maintaining our witness by seeming serene and saying what's appropriate, that we internalize grief. I've been with people who have suddenly lost a family member, and they are about ready to lose their cool and give God a piece of their mind for taking their spouse or child. Then they remember that the preacher is standing within ear shot. "I know that God will make something good out of my tragedy," the distraught person says with a sad smile.

Sure, I know that he will, too. But I also know that at that moment the person needs to lay out a complaint against God openly and passionately. The preacher won't be offended, or at least shouldn't be. God certainly won't take offense. Perhaps our inmost being doesn't boast in the Lord as it should because we have unresolved grief and anger from past crises. Boasting bespeaks personal intimate connection. I don't brag about the accomplishments of someone I don't know. But I will rejoice and tell the accomplishments of my wife and children. And after dealing with some serious interpersonal issues between the Lord and me over my probable ALS diagnosis, I am able to boast in the Lord.

The fourth Hebrew word used to describe the praise of God is *glorify*: "Glorify the LORD with me." The word *glorify*, meaning to lift up or make great, is actually a word of measurement. The Bible uses a word that is translated "priest," for example, and another word translated "high priest." The word used for *high* is the same as that used for *glorify*. The Bible, too, uses a word for "mountain" and also uses a word for "high mountain." Again, the word *high* is the word for *glorify*. The word for glorify differentiates between a priest and a greater priest, that is, the high priest; it differentiates between a mountain and a greater mountain, that is, the high mountain. When we glorify God, then, we declare that God is greater, lifting up God as greater than anything that we know, anything that we can measure, anything that we can experience or understand. We say, "God, you are greater!"

The fifth word that can be translated "praise" is *exalt*: "Let us exalt his name together." The verb *exalt* means to put someone at the highest possible level. When we exalt the name of God, we place him at the highest possible level, declaring that he is the King of kings and Lord of lords. There is no one above him and there is no one to compare to him.

The power of praise

Praising God is to acknowledge him as our only source of blessing, power, and hope. It means to passionately and with zeal turn the spotlight on God and illuminate his character for all to see, to lift God up above the rubble of our lives and the brokenness all around us. It means to lift him above our fears, our shame, our evil, our brokenness, and our crushed spirits, to place God in the only position he deserves— high and lifted up. Praising God is our challenge no matter what circumstances we face.

Perhaps you're thinking, "It's fine to praise God, but what good will it do? What good will it do for those who lost loved ones on September 11? What good will it do for those whose lives have fallen apart? Isn't praising God an exercise in futility?" Note the advice of the psalmist: "My soul will boast in the LORD; let the afflicted hear and rejoice" (Psalm 34:2). When we praise God, something miraculous happens: Others who are also afflicted respond and find joy.

Evil comes in many forms. In the World Trade Center and Pentagon attacks, evil came from personal evildoers with hateful motives. Having a motor neuron disease is another sort of evil, a part of the degradation and corruption of life that came with the fall of mankind. Disasters and devastation always have an evil element in that they cause pain. They are not God's best for his creation. They are futility and frustration. And the pain they cause reaches into every corner of our world. Christians know the source of evil better than do others, because we have God's revealed truth about it. We, of all people, should deal with it honestly and candidly. We are not naive Pollyannas who need to find "happy thoughts" in order to survive.

Survive we will, for it is true—when we meet disaster face to face, the God who never changes is always with us. We can face those fears, because God is always in control. Such are the reasons to praise God. And, truly, there is healing power in the praise of our God.